THE SHOT HEARD AROUND THE WORLD

How I Went from The Playground To The White House

Dereck Whittenburg

Testimony from Pam Valvano-Strasser

Pam Valvano-Strasser and daughters

It is hard to describe what Dereck has meant to me and the Valvano family. When we arrived in North Carolina, Dereck and the other players became our family. The relationship was truly unique. The year 1983 was more than I could ever have imagined. The last nine NCAA games were magical. It was so special that no one ever thought we could win. The players would tell me that Jim would have them practice cutting down the Nets until it became a reality when they won the 1983 National Championship. The "30 for 30" film that Dereck produced was special to me and so many people in the country. To this day, people still come up to me and talk about it. What I remember most about Dereck is that anytime he calls the house, he always says, "Pam, this is your son." Having him in our family made our relationship so special to me. He helped to make Jim's dream come true. Jim would be so proud of what he has done with his life after the championship. Thank you, Dereck, for everything you have done for Jim and the family. Love, Mom.

Testimony from Dick Vitale (Award Winning ESPN and Hall of Fame Commentator)

I think the National Championship in 1983 inspired many to chase their dreams. It proved that you could achieve success with DESIRE and DEDICATION. Because of my life in college basketball, it was one of the greatest stories in sports. People must realize it was a very dramatic situation to get into the Big Dance, the NCAA tournament, and play in March Madness. First, they had to beat two of the greatest teams in the nation to survive and enter the national tournament. Then, they had to beat a terrific University of North Carolina team led by the spectacular Michael Jordan. They followed that with an incredible win over Virginia's highly-rated superb squad led by National Player of the Year Ralph Sampson. Once in the tournament, it was fighting in each game for survival and ultimately standing tall with the gold trophy as the 1983 National Champs. Dereck Whittenburg was a player who loved the Big Moment! He performed his best on the biggest stage and was always TEAM-oriented. He was a genuine winner in the Game of Life and showed a winning mentality in leading the Wolfpack to a National Championship in 1983. Jim Valvano was a born leader, possessing a "golden gift" in communicating his theories and concepts to his team. Jimmy's personality was infectious and became contagious with all he encountered. He dreamed of winning a national title and magnificently got his players to think positively and believe it could be a reality. His dream ultimately came true in 1983, and Jim Valvano's leadership now affects millions of people with the dollars raised through the V Foundation for Cancer Research. The 30/30 film SURVIVE AND ADVANCE showed a team with great camaraderie and a team that loved competing together to achieve the goal of winning a national championship. SURVIVE AND ADVANCE was well done and received national acclaim for its production. Seeing the incredible mental toughness and love between each player who wore the Wolfpack uniform made it special. The movie production was first-class in every way, and it showed what a team playing together can achieve with a mindset of believing in one another.

Testimony from GEORGE BODENHEIMER (President, ESPN (1998-2011) Executive Chairman (2012-2014)

For a lot of people, winning the National Championship would be the defining moment of their lives. For Dereck Whittenburg, it was just the beginning as he has led a life of purpose by helping others. In "The Shot Heard Around the World," you'll learn how he always found a way to rise to the occasion…whether it was by winning the Championship in '83 or producing one of ESPN's most viewed documentaries "Survive and Advance" or by impacting the lives of so many by creating the "Dereck Whittenburg

Foundation" as well as by serving on the board of the V Foundation for Cancer Research.

Testimony from Tommy Amaker (Former Duke Basketball Star under Hall of Famer Coach Krzyzewski & current Head Basketball Coach at Harvard University)

I've known Dereck for a long, long time. Both of us hail from the DC area, so I was aware of Dereck before knowing him personally. I admired him from a distance, beginning in his high school years at DeMatha. He's one of those guys that is infectious when you get to know the spirit of Dereck. He's tough and has unwavering confidence. It's a gift he has in his belief in himself and others. He's been highly successful in every facet of his life. I'm a big admirer and happy to say a friend.

The 1983 National Championship game ended with one of the most incredible finishes in sports history, especially collegiate sports. As such, NC State was a team that showed astonishing toughness and resilience. People saw the journey's end and thought it was always supposed to be that way. This story will give you great insight into how it all came together; this was such an improbable run to a National Championship and a historic one. When they rank historic finishes, I can't imagine that Dereck Whittenburg's "pass" to Lorenzo Charles isn't on that list. I need to figure out where to rank it, but it would be on that list. I still picture Coach V running around the court when they had that historic, improbable finish at the buzzer. I also think of Valvano's famous speech at the Espy Awards when he was battling cancer. 'Don't give up, don't ever give up'...motivational. Coach V was brilliant. Here was a man who could do so many things; being a basketball coach just happened to be one of them. We are so lucky that he was a basketball coach. We are also lucky to have experienced everything he accomplished for the game of basketball. Coach Valvano and the 1983 North Carolina State National Championship team left a great legacy in collegiate basketball.

Testimony from Terry Gannon (1983 Championship Teammate and Sportscaster for NBC Sports and Golf Channel)

Nobody outside our locker room believed we would win the 1983 National Championship game. I had family members who took Houston and laid the points. But our coach, Jim Valvano, told us he believed. Our senior leaders, including Dereck Whittenburg, refused to let us believe anything else. Pulling off the impossible took a Hail Mary "pass" and a buzzer-beating dunk. How'd we do it? We bought into THE TEAM! It took everybody, all of us, to climb that mountain. In this book, Dereck reminds us that we all have people who give us the great gift of belief in our careers and lives. He has long been one of those people for me!

Table of Contents

Chapter 1

Our Obligation

As I get older, I have come to terms with figuring out what Coach Valvano was trying to teach me. He had been trying to teach me what life and our legacy are about. He taught me that life is about helping others to find their dream. It's not about what kind of house you have or what car you drive, but rather, it's all about spending time with people who need a little uplifting and encouragement to make their dreams come true. That's what you're supposed to be doing. That's what your legacy should be. It doesn't matter how smart you are or how much better you are compared to others. What matters most in life is that you help others in need. Yes, we won the 1983 National Championship at NC State, where you see Coach Valvano running around the court celebrating, but at the end of the day, his legacy isn't about being a champion. It's about helping people fight cancer. That's powerful stuff. That's bigger than us. That's why we compete every day. We are all on the same team, competing to help others. There is nothing healthier than that. That's what makes life fun. Coach Valvano and I built a great relationship from the day we met until his passing in 1993 because of our bond. When you think of him, you will probably also think of me. It's like when you think of Jordan and Pippen,

Shaq and Kobe, or Ali and Joe Frazier. You can only have a conversation by bringing up the other.

What made our relationship different from any of those analogies is that you may never find a coach/player relationship like ours. Everyone remembers the incredible connection we had. You can talk about any coach or team that has won a championship but will never struggle with remembering who won the 1983 Championship and who the coach was. You will remember the memorable moment when the game ended. Being part of that team was great, but I wanted to share my story with the world to see how my journey may relate to yours. We all have choices and decisions to make in life. But to make it to where we want to be, you must be willing to listen and work hard for it. For most people, nothing in life falls in your lap. It would help if you took full advantage of the many great opportunities presented to you to pursue your dreams and accomplish whatever you set out to become. Life itself doesn't just pick who will be the next star or who will become successful. Discipline is key. Without discipline, your vision will eventually become just an illusion. Throughout this book, you will read about the importance of making positive decisions, having positive people around you, how to be a great teammate, why you should respect your elders, and most importantly, realizing that your resiliency and the ability to overcome some of your biggest obstacles is part of life. Are you going to struggle or fail sometimes? Absolutely. Struggles are an integral part of growth. The important thing is that you don't give up. You get up every day and keep trying until you reach where you want to be. You go out, find your happiness, and then use your experience to push others until they find theirs. As Coach Valvano used to say, "Never Give Up!" That's what life is about.

Chapter 2

The Whittenburgs

My last name isn't a common name you hear daily. It is also a very rare name for a Black person. In fact, when you hear the name Whittenburg, I'm pretty sure the first thing that will cross your mind is that it is not a person of color. No one has ever asked me where the last name came from. However, while it is a rare name for a Black person, I know the origin of my name. As I hope this book will show you, I am very proud of my name, its origins, and what my family had to overcome to create a better story from the origins in which it came from.

The origin of my last name, Whittenburg, comes from Austria. While researching the name, I found some very interesting information. According to some citizens of German and Austrian descent, the word *wit* or *witt* was used in Middle Low German, and it means white. The word *berg* means mountains. Together, it means "white mountain." However, in Grimms Dictionary, the word wit stands for forest or wood, and from that noun comes the word Witten, which means to collect (fire) wood. Together, the name is spelled Wittenberg, which means a place known as a firewood collection mountain. As I dug a little deeper into the meaning of my last name, I also found that Wittenberg is a town in Germany where, on

October 31, 1517, priest Martin Luther read the Wittenberg Articles and then nailed his 95 Theses to the door of the Castle Church and the Protestant Reformation began. The town's official name is Lutherstadt-Wittenberg.

If you notice, the word and the town's name are spelled differently from my last name, which is spelled Whittenburg. According to my family, our last name came from two brothers who were slave owners who had migrated from Germany to Virginia and then settled in South Carolina. According to one of my uncles, the Wittenbergs fell on hard times and sold their slaves to a family by the last name Clay, who were from South Carolina. After noticing that the Clay family were not good owners and mistreated their slaves, the Wittenbergs took the slaves back. Once they took back ownership of their slaves, they changed the spelling of their last name to Whittenburg. I wish I knew the rest of the story because I'm pretty sure there is more to it, but that's what has been shared with me over the years. I do know there are 1500 slave graves of Whittenbergs in Gaffney, South Carolina dating back to the 1800s.

Many more important and interesting historical events are tied to the last name Whittenburg. Although his last name is spelled slightly differently from mine, AJ Whittenberg, a civil rights leader responsible for integrating schools in the 1960s, is my relative. A new elementary school named AJ Whittenberg Elementary School of Engineering opened in 2010 that is in downtown Greenville, South Carolina. AJ, whose real name was Abraham Jonah Whittenberg was born in 1918 and was one of fourteen children. At the age of 16, he moved to Simpsonville to attend St. Alban's Training School, where he graduated in 1931. He later opened his own gas service station in Greenville but was forced to shut down his business due to his civil rights activities.

Abraham Jonah Whittenberg

Whittenberg, who was the president of the Greenville NAACP in 1959, hosted baseball legend Jackie Robinson to speak at the South Carolina

NAACP conference. When Jackie Robinson and other African Americans were threatened with arrests for sitting in a *"whites only"* section at the Greenville Airport, Whittenberg helped organize a major march that attracted national attention. Other Whittenbergs participated in the civil rights movement, including AJ's son, AJ Whittenberg Jr., who was arrested for demonstrating against segregation in 1960. Then, in 1963, Whittenberg and his attorneys filed a lawsuit that allowed his daughter, Elaine, to transfer schools and become one of the first African American students to desegregate Greenville schools in 1964.

There's also a Wittenberg University in Ohio, which is a Division 3 school. Upon doing further research, I was also able to find other relatives who came from the Whittenburgs. When it comes to the Family Tree, there are four championship connections. David Thompson's mother, Ida Gentry Thompson Davis's grandmother, Etta Whittenburg, is my grandfather's sister. David Thompson, who played on the 1974 North Carolina State National Championship team, has a niece, Charlotte Smith, who won the 1994 National Championship at North Carolina. We have Alvin Gentry, whose father, Geter Gentry, is David's mother's brother. Alvin Gentry won in 1988 as an assistant coach under Larry Brown at the University of Kansas. I also have a cousin named Darnell Whittenburg, a very good Olympian specializing in rings, vault, and floor who grew up in Baltimore. Then, of course, myself.

Although the last name had been given to us by slave owners, I have to say that I am very proud of what my family had to overcome to create a better story from the origins from which it came. I am very proud to say that my family was strong enough to not only survive those critical times but also manage to migrate from the South to escape the trauma that slavery and racism caused. There is still a lot of history that I am unaware of when it comes to my family back in the South. Still, because of their willingness to never give up while striving for a better life and greater opportunities, they taught me the meaning of what sacrifice and determination really are.

I would not be who or what I am today had it not been for the teachings of not just my parents but also all the caring and nurturing people who played a major part in helping me throughout my journey, at its essence. The Whittenburg story is about a family striving to survive and advance. Before anything else, I want to thank all of you who helped pave the way for me to accomplish the many great things I have been able to do. Because of all of you, I am very proud to call myself a member of the *Whittenburg* family.

Chapter 3

Pivotal Moment

Because of the lack of opportunities in the South, many would leave their children behind with their grandparents so they could go and seek better jobs in the North. In some cases, the children would go months, if not years, without being able to see their parents. Although it might have been for the better, I can't imagine the hurt and pain some of those children must have gone through in those tough times. But that was the sacrifice people had to make to be able to provide for their families. I'm sure many kids throughout history were left with an empty space in their hearts, causing them to be affected all the way through their adult lives. I was one of the lucky ones who didn't have to endure that pain. However, I understand why caring mothers and fathers had to make some tough sacrifices in those difficult times.

My mother, Lillian Hubert, was born in Atmore, Alabama. After graduating high school, she began working at the farm like everyone else did in the South. Her oldest brother, George Hubert, and his wife, Mary, were the first to migrate from the South and into the Washington DC area near The Capitol in the mid-1950s. My aunt Mary was a manager at a Hot Shoppes diner, an upscale diner owned by a J.W. Marriott. Being that she was running the restaurant, she would always try and encourage other relatives from back home to come and stay with her and work until they were able to afford to live on their own. My mother, not wanting to get stuck out there working the farms, took her up on the offer and decided to move up North to Washington, DC, with them. Once she could get on her feet, she called for her other family members to come and live with her until they could also move out on their own.

My Parents, Don & Lilian Whittenburg, and Aunt Olivia

Uncle George Hubert and Aunt Mary Hubert

My mom and Uncle George were both outstanding basketball players and good shooters. My mom was a standout player for the Escambia County Training School basketball team in Atmore, Alabama, the only high school black people could attend. Not only was she a great player, but she was also the captain of the team. My Uncle George and Aunt Mary had also played basketball in high school back in Atmore, Alabama. In 1956, my uncle George Hubert, who was stationed at Fort Belvoir Army Base in Alexandria, Virginia, became the first black player for the basketball team.

Members of the Fort Belvoir basketball team which met Bolling AFB for its opener last night. Knee(?) (left to right): Ed Dzubak, Ken Garrity, Milt Papke, Dick Ursem, Conrad Deritis, Joe Loprete, (?) trainer Howard Juvinall(?) ... : Coach Dale Seymour, trainer Don Lander, George Hubbert, Jac(?) ...olds, Bob Wage...(?) Harmon Hoffmann, John Fehily and trainer Red Schroeder ...

Fort Belvoir Base Basketball Team

So, basketball was in my bloodline from my mother's side of the family. My Aunt Mary said my mother was our family's best basketball player. It was in my DNA. My father, Don Whittenburg, from Gaffney, South Carolina, was in the reserves and stationed at the Fort Belvoir Army Base, where my Uncle George happened to be his sergeant. My uncle George had invited my father over to his house for dinner one day, and that's how he and my mother met. My father had a son named Steven, who is 3 years older than me, from a previous relationship he had been in while living in Gaffney. My parents eventually began dating, and they married after a couple of years. After working at Hot Shoppes for a couple of years, my mother later found a better-paying job as a social worker for the government. She helped families and individuals who needed government assistance and worked there until she retired.

I was born on October 2, 1960, at Providence Hospital in Washington, DC. My sister Wanda was born in 1963, and 8 years later, my brother Reginald was born in 1971. We lived in an apartment building near 16th Street in the Southeast district near the Frederick Douglas house and not too far from where the late Legendary Georgetown Hoyas Head Coach John Thompson resided. I only know where he lived because I read it in his book, "I Came as A Shadow," years later when I became an adult. After playing a short stint with the Boston Celtics behind the great Bill Russell, he returned to the DC area to coach at St. Anthony's before becoming the head coach at Georgetown University. John Thompson and my high school coach, Morgan Wootten, were rivals at one point but could never schedule a game against each other because they couldn't get the terms right. Coach Wootten didn't want to play in DC, and Coach Thompson didn't want to play in Maryland. When the Georgetown position as head coach came up, Coach Wootten, who was coaching at DeMatha High School then, wanted the job, but John Thompson ended up getting the job over him. They both had great coaching careers and were enshrined in the Naismith Basketball Hall of Fame. By the early age of 5 years old, I was already running around outside playing pickup games like baseball. basketball and sandlot football. I remember these kids in my neighborhood as the Williams brothers, who became good friends of mine. Out of all the sports we played, baseball was my favorite. The Williams brothers and I dreamed of putting together all the money we had saved and going to Sears to buy some baseball equipment. Financially wise, baseball is a sport requiring a lot more equipment. The only problem was making it to Sears to purchase it. To get to Sears, we had to walk through Berry Farms, a dangerous area notorious for being a hangout for some of the neighborhood's biggest bullies. Those bullies were a lot older than we were and they would pick on anyone who crossed their path. On several occasions, I personally got to witness some pretty intense moments where those bullies roughed up and went through the pockets of some of my friends who tried walking through their territory. I was the smallest kid out of all of us, so after observing that the bullies would only attempt to rob the bigger kids, my friends became wise and started putting the money in my pockets instead. The plan eventually worked out for us, and we could finally get past them to buy the equipment we needed to play. During the summertime, my mother always brought me to visit my grandparents back in Alabama. My grandparents lived on a farm out in the country. I wasn't used to seeing so much land because when you're used to living in the city, you don't have all that open space. When I went down there, I used to run around all day to the point where my grandfather would say, "What's wrong with that kid?" One of the things I remember about when we used to go down to Alabama was there were no bathrooms with a toilet inside the house. They had what they called an outhouse, which looked like a Porta Potty, only made of wood. Then, according to my oldest brother Steve, when we would go and visit my dad's sister, Aunt Olivia, in Virginia, he says I was the craziest kid he had ever seen because of the way I would jump off the top of the old car that she had parked outside in her yard and fall to the ground. When he thought I was hurt, I kept getting back up and running around. Everyone used to say I was the most energetic kid they had ever seen because I was always running around. Growing up in DC, my father often drove down Pennsylvania Avenue, and I would get a close view of the White House. Every time we drove past it, I wondered what it must feel like to be inside the most powerful place in the world. I remember always saying, "Wow, that's where the president lives." As a kid, that was a big time for me. While other kids may have dreamed of becoming an athlete or entertainer, mine was to become the President of the United States. It was just a cool thing to say, even though I had no idea what the President's job was. I believe it was because I was so used to driving by the White House that it became the simplest ambition I could develop. We lived in the DC area until I was eight years old. 1968 was the most pivotal moment in my life that I could remember. Out of all my memories from my childhood, it was the year that Dr. Martin Luther King Jr. was assassinated. I didn't know anything about Martin Luther King other than that he was a civil rights leader and a national personality fighting for equal rights for all people. I used to enjoy sitting in front of our television and hearing him speak because Dr. King was so wise and eloquent. He was the first black person I saw on television who had notoriety from my perspective back in the 60's. He was just such a magnetic figure. Dr. King's speeches were so dynamic that it was difficult not to be drawn to him. One of the moments I cherish the most was his impactful "I Have a Dream Speech." Although I was too young to know the entire meaning behind the speech fully, I knew that he was a man of equality and was well respected by many. The assassination of Dr. King was such a shocking moment in time. I didn't know why it happened, and my parents didn't discuss it. I believe that everyone had become so numb by it that they couldn't even come up with the words to talk about what had occurred. Once the news began to spread around the country about Dr. King's assassination, people started rioting, setting fires everywhere, looting, and robbing everything in sight. It was the wrong time to be in Washington, DC.

Before the assassination, my mother always reminded me to close the door anytime I ran outside to play because there were times when I would forget. One day, as I was walking off my porch and down my steps to go out and play with my friend Ronald Williams, I noticed these two guys walking past me and heading towards our door. You could tell by how they looked around that they were up to no good. When they reached the door, they began attempting to wedge their way into the house but were unsuccessful because I remembered to lock it. After becoming frustrated that they couldn't get in the house, one turned around and asked me if anyone was inside. I told them that no one was home then, and within minutes, they turned and walked away. Once I saw they were gone, my friend Ronald and I ran to his house and called the police. My mother had no idea what had occurred until I returned to our house to tell her.

Luckily, nothing happened that day because I had listened to my mother and locked our door. Lord only knows what could have happened that day had I forgotten to lock it. A couple of weeks before that incident, someone snatched my mother's purse while she was making her way home. It just so happened that we later found out that the same guys who were trying to break into our house were the same guys who had snatched my mother's purse. They had gotten our address from my mother's identification card in her purse. Back then, it was standard for thieves to run up to women and take off with their purses. But things just continued getting worse around DC as time went on to the point where my parents began discussing their plans to move into a more peaceful environment because of how dangerous and violent things had become after the assassination. The dream back then for most families, particularly for Black families, was to one day be able to purchase their own house. Again, not to make it about race, but during the 1950s, America was 90% White, and our generation hadn't built wealth. That became even more of an urgent situation for my parents because of how violent DC had become after the riots. When my father received the G.I. Bill, it made it possible for my parents to afford to buy our own house finally. That allowed us to begin shopping for a home. I remember when my parents used to take me along with them through neighborhoods and look at houses that were up for sale. In 1969, they found the one they fell in love with and purchased their first home in Glenarden, Maryland, in Prince George's County in a predominantly Black middle-class neighborhood. Prince George's County is one of the wealthiest black counties in the country. It's one of the most affluent because most blacks hired to work a government job would move there from the DC area when they wanted to purchase a home. It was a different experience to go from living in an apartment to having more room in a bigger house. It was a significant accomplishment for my parents because we were now living in a much more peaceful and safer environment than in DC, where we were beginning to outgrow the apartment where we lived and needed more room for our family. I spent much time with my little brother Reggie as a young kid. He was like my little sidekick. Aside from my father being in the reserves, he was also a mechanic working at the BMW dealership in Alexandria, Virginia, about 20 minutes from our house. The area where we lived was also known as the DMV, which stood for DC,

Maryland, and Virginia because of how close in proximity all three were. During the summertime, my dad would often take me to work with him, and that's where I landed my first ever job washing cars at nine years old. I don't remember getting paid much, but it was a good experience for me to be around the older kids who also worked there.

My parents were big on discipline at home. Today, when I give motivational speeches, one of the first things I mention to the crowd is that we all have much in common. I ask, "How many of you ever got a Whipping?" I would see everyone raise their hands. I would ask, "How many of you got two Whippings?" Most times, I would see everyone raise their hands again. By the time I got to ask how many of them had ever gotten a third Whipping, there would always be fewer hands raised, and that's because, after those first two Whippings, you would have learned your lesson to avoid getting your third one. All I had to hear was, "Wait until your daddy gets home" or "Go and get me the switch" for me to straighten up. Parenting is much different nowadays.

My mother has always been an excellent cook. Her meals were very special to me. She made the best fried chicken in the world and baked the best sweet potato pies I have ever tasted. I remember that we always used to gather around and eat together at the dinner table, which many people have gotten away from these days. One day, my mother made some beautiful, great-tasting pork chops, and I went over and got two pork chops for myself, but because I had gotten full having just one of them, I threw the other one in the unlined trash can and ran outside to play. When I came back inside, I could tell my father wasn't in a good mood judging by the look on his face. "Come here, son," he says as he leads me into the kitchen and straight to the trash. First, let me explain this: back then when you looked in the garbage, there was no bag where you would toss things away. All you saw was gook and a bunch of junk. When my father opened the trash bin, all I saw was that beautiful pork chop sitting right on top. He pointed at it and asked me, "Didn't you ask for that pork chop?" Nervously, I responded, "Yes." He said, "Take it out of there, put it on a plate, and eat it while I sit here and watch you." Not to mention, he also had a belt lying right there on top of the table. I ate that whole pork chop in just a few minutes. After that, I never left anything else on my plate. That was one of the many valuable lessons I learned growing up. Throughout my life, I have been continuously blessed with valuable lessons from my parents and countless others who believe in me.

Back then, our parents were very upfront and told us the truth, and so did our coaches. There was no sugarcoating it. They said what they said, and they moved on. The one thing I can remember about my parents is that they never talked about race or politics. I never once heard "The white man is going to do this" or "because of the color of your skin," there was none of that. Those types of conversations never took place in our home. Everything was all about what we needed to do and how we needed to achieve it. They never talked about any ill will regarding their past experiences. When it came to teaching moments, they would never lecture me by using examples of how things were when they were growing up. They always dealt with situations as they occurred. If they had to discipline me, they would spank me and go on about their business. They weren't the type to say things like "My parents did this" or "When I was a kid" as an example to try to teach me to understand what they had been through. They never threw those types of things in my face. I always felt their unconditional love regarding the valuable lessons they were trying to teach me through discipline.

There are times when I felt I should have asked them more questions regarding their experience of how things were when they were younger, but at the same time, I'm not sure how any lectures involving their situations would have helped me today. I'm happy that they were always optimistic about raising me. I will always appreciate my parents for choosing a better environment to raise us in; I'm not sure what my life would be like today had it not been for their decision to move. When they were younger, they left the South around the time of the brutal murder of Emmett Till. Part of their decision to migrate might have also been the Jim Crow Laws. You've got to remember that when they were younger, times were very hard for Blacks in the South, and there weren't any great job opportunities for them back then. There was also a fear factor when it came to racism. But my parents did their best to make sure they protected me from the very same things they fought to overcome.

I wanted to share my journey with the world to talk about what I accomplished and show how important it is to acknowledge all the people who came along and played a big part in making it all possible. I wanted to use my story to deliver an impactful message to help many understand that life doesn't always go as planned. However, there are so many other options for you to succeed. Today, when I go around the country and speak, I speak in relative terms because it's a technique I have always used throughout my career. Many kids have these big dreams of becoming an athlete or entertainer. What they never stop to think about is that 99.9% of the people who think just like them will never make it. But that shouldn't be considered a negative because 99.9% will become successful at becoming something other than an athlete or entertainer. That is relative success. Like Coach Valvano always said, "A group of ordinary people can achieve extraordinary things." That's what our 1983 National Championship was about. However successful we were in basketball, most of those players also became champions in other industries. That is relative success.

I came up with the idea to write my story when I first started the Dereck Whittenburg Foundation in 2015, but I didn't just want to write a book to write it. I wanted to write a bestseller with a powerful message. I wanted everyone who picked up my book to say it was a great read, that they got something impactful out of it, and that it motivated them to continue to pursue their dreams. The Dereck Whittenburg Foundation's mission is to extend financial assistance to deserving college students who face financial hardships while completing their college degrees/education. Our mantra is "Dream. Believe. Work. Now Finish!" We aim to support juniors and seniors attending North Carolina colleges and universities to graduate with lower student debt. I have experienced many significant moments that many people can relate to and gravitate to. I know how hard it is to reach where you want to be, but I also understand that life doesn't end when dreams don't come true. It just means you must find another avenue to take in life to survive and provide for your family.

When most people hear the name Dereck Whittenburg, they will likely remember me as one of the players who participated in one of the most memorable championship games in NCAA history. And I get that. For many years, I felt trapped in this box where many will only bring up that memory. I do not want to take away from that historical moment because it was a great moment in sports history. But I want people to understand that it was the door that might have opened for me to have many more opportunities once my basketball career ended; it's just not all of who I am. There is so much more behind the player that many people don't know about. I tell everyone, "It's not like I've been standing out there on the curb holding up a sign with my jersey bragging about winning the 1983 National Championship for the past 40 years". I had to continue my life from that moment and accomplish many other things. Although I loved many things about Coach John Thompson's book, one part always stuck with me, which I use anytime I go out and speak to the youth. In one of his chapters, he mentions that he had a completely flat basketball on his desk in his office. When the kids entered his office, he explained why the flat basketball was there. He would tell them that there won't be any air in the ball someday because sports will eventually be over for them. It was just such an excellent example for kids to have a visual of what he was trying to express to them.

There are so many who have no idea that I am an award-winning filmmaker or that I have been a motivational speaker. I understand that, too, but this is my opportunity to try and reach as many of the people who may not only be curious about who I am but also those seeking any wisdom to help them along their path in life; this is the whole story of Dereck Cornelious Whittenburg and not just the television NC State 1983 National Championship Dereck Whittenburg; this is a story I felt should be written for the 99.9% who are not successful when it comes to sports or entertainment. Although I was a great athlete who didn't make it as a professional athlete at one point in my life, I learned to use sports to become successful at helping others; that's what the other purpose of sports should be. I am telling my story to encourage people to accomplish their goals and remind them to always remember to give credit to those involved throughout their journey.

Chapter 4

The Playground

Going to a new school in Maryland was a different experience for me. I went from attending an all-black elementary school in DC to being enrolled at integrated Glenarden Elementary School. Although it was my first time sitting in a classroom with students of different ethnicities, it seemed comfortable. It was no big deal to me. It just made me a little curious. I went to Ketchup Elementary for one year and then transferred to Moulton Elementary School just down the road, where I attended for 5th grade. And guess what? When I got to the 6th grade at Glenarden Woods Elementary School, my music teacher, Ms. Harris, asked me what I wanted to be when I got older. I told her I wanted to become the President of the United States. Besides being well-behaved and having fun with other students, I don't remember much from my elementary school days. Since I was now old enough to play at the Boys and Girls Club, my parents signed me up. That's when I learned about playing organized sports. I was bigger than other kids my age, and sports at the Boys and Girls Club went by weight. Because of my size, I could never play with kids my age. I always had to go and play with the older kids. When the kids would ask me my name, I would tell them it is Dereck Whittenburg; they would respond, "Whitten what? Your new name is "Tweety Bird," so due to the playground, I've been stuck with the nickname ever since. No one in Glenarden ever acknowledged me by my real name until I entered high school. At this point in my life, people used to say I had an attitude and was a hothead when it came to competing. It didn't matter what games we played; I always played to win. Initially, I didn't know that basketball would be the sport I would eventually fall in love with and choose over the others I played. I was just out there running around and enjoying whatever we decided to play that day and having fun. The first organized team sport I ever played was baseball. My first-ever coach was Mr. Brown, who lived right down the street from me. He thought I was an outstanding baseball player but quickly realized I had a little temper. I recall that during one of our games, a pitch hit me on my shoulder, and after taking a few steps down the first baseline, I decided to go and run after the opposing pitcher instead. Our first base coach, Mr. Swindell, caught up to me from behind and held me back before I could reach the mound to fight the pitcher. I was thrown out of the game and had to sit out the next game as a punishment. I'm sure the pitcher wasn't trying to hit me intentionally but growing up as an athlete and a tough kid, I was always ready to fight anybody at any moment. Also, because of my size, I always felt like I could go around and beat anyone up. I remember being out at one of the local parks and playing a pickup game of basketball with a few kids from around my neighborhood, and for some reason, I began picking on one of the kids we were playing against, who was much older than me. He had become fed up with all the trash-talking I was doing, and he ended up coming after me, and we got into a fight. Not only was he older than I was, but he was also much bigger and stronger. He was pounding on me so hard that all I could do was try and cover myself the best I could. He ended up getting me pretty good. That was the first time I experienced a beatdown! From that fight, I quickly learned that there would always be someone out there who could beat you up no matter how big and tough you thought you were. There was another time when my mouth caused me to get into even bigger trouble. I reached my weight limit when I was about 13 or 14 years old and played in my final season as a Boys and Girls Club football player under Coach Earl Gray. We were out there on Glenarden Field right by the Recreational Center, and during practice, my good friend Keith Lynch and I were having a punting contest to determine who would be the team's punter. We both put up some good kicks, and after going at it for a while, I felt I had beaten him out for the position. Coach Gray decided to award the position to Keith instead. And yet again, because of my temper and not being able to control myself, I shouted out, "Shit," I'm a much better punter than this guy." I said it loud enough for Coach Gray to hear me. That single curse word got me suspended from the team for the entire season.

Back Row #42

I could continue practicing and stand on the sidelines while wearing my uniform, but I was not allowed to go in and play. The punishment seemed harsh, but my coach felt he had to teach me a valuable lesson. Most of the players on the team were very upset about it because I was one of the best players, and they all felt we could have won the championship that year. Although I was trying out to be the punter, I also played multiple positions like tight end, linebacker, and fullback. My coaches and teammates said I was a good all-around player. But none of that mattered to the coach. Standing on the sideline and being unable to play bothered me because of how competitive I was. Most of our games were on Saturday, and my father often came to see me play. He wasn't the type who would yell and scream like some of the other parents, so most of the time, I really didn't even know he was there because he was so quiet. One of the best things that I can say about my parents when it came to me playing sports is that they never questioned or got involved in any of my coaches' decisions on the field. Unlike these days where most parents get too wrapped up with and interfering with the coaches' decisions.

After not playing a single down the entire season, Coach Gray walked over to me in our last game and said to me *"Tweety Bird, go in."* I remember becoming so emotional that I started crying as I ran onto the field from the excitement of finally being able to go out there and play. I didn't care that it was our last game. I was just happy that he had finally put me in. Looking back, I truly feel that he wanted to use my punishment as a lesson to show the entire team that if he could sit out one of the best players on the team that he would do the same to any of them.

I'll tell you what though, I never heard any of my teammates say another curse word in front of the coach that entire year. Having to sit out not only taught me a great lesson, but it also helped me with my discipline moving forward. By this time, I had already given up playing baseball because the better I got at it, the more difficult it became to find where to play. In other words, if I wanted to continue playing baseball, it meant that I would have to play on a travel team. Besides, most of the kids in my neighborhood weren't playing baseball at my level so I lost all my interest in wanting to continue playing and began focusing more on playing basketball. After the football season ended, I went on to play in my final season at Boys and Girls Club before going into my first year in junior high.

My first basketball lesson came from an unexpected source. I remember Coach Carter, one of the coaches at the Boys and Girls Club, always chastising me and telling me that I needed to work on my free throws. I was a pretty cocky kid back then and would always respond by telling him, "I'm already good at my free throws, coach; *I don't need to work on them."* Until then, I had never seen my mother play basketball, even though I had heard stories about how great she was when she was younger. My mother stood about 5'9, tall for a woman, and played basketball in high school. When Coach Carter saw her enter the gym to pick me up, he said,

"I bet your mom would beat you in a free throw contest." He knew something about my mother that I didn't know about basketball. I looked at him like he was crazy because there was no way I would have ever let my mother beat me. After practice, while the entire team watched, my mother went up to the free-throw line and made 14 out of 15 shots. I remember saying, *"Oh wow, my mom can shoot."* She ended up beating me because I only made 12 out of 15. From that moment on I made sure to always practice my free throws. I learned many lessons listening to my coaches, but it took some prompting, a yearlong suspension, and schooling from my mother in this case. This was when I first saw my cousin and idol David Thompson play. He was playing at North Carolina State, and it was his first nationally televised game where he scored 28 points against the University of Maryland. Honestly, I had no idea I was even related to him. It wasn't until halfway through the game that my dad said, *"You know David Thompson is your cousin."* Hearing my dad tell me that changed my life. From then on, I knew I wanted to be a basketball player. Not only was David a great player who I enjoyed watching, but I was even more excited knowing we were related. I remember going to the bus stop on my way to school, bragging, and telling everyone *David Thompson* is my cousin. No one ever believed me, though. But I didn't care because I knew he was definitely related to me. Because of him, I wanted to grow up and become a basketball player myself. Back then, the ACC was the only conference that was regularly airing games live on television on Raycom Sports every Saturday morning and I always made sure I always watched all the games. That was my introduction to ACC basketball. After that, I always looked forward to watching him play every Saturday morning. I still remember watching him win the 1974 National Championship at NC State and saying, "I want to go to NC State and win one, *too."* In the early to mid-70s, college basketball was more prevalent than the NBA, and David Thompson was *that guy.* But Thompson was not just one of the greatest players to ever play in the ACC and win a National Championship, he also went on to become a star NBA player for the

Denver Nuggets and the Seattle Supersonics. He is one of the 8 players to score 70 or more points in an NBA game and was later inducted into the Naismith Basketball Hall of Fame in 1996. He was such a legend that even Michael Jordan, who was two years younger than me then, used to look up to him and, years later, even picked David to present him in the Basketball Hall of Fame.

With David Thompson

After Elementary school, I attended William Wirt Junior High School in Riverdale Park, Maryland, which required kids from my neighborhood to take a bus across town and pick up different kids from other neighborhoods. I did recognize some of the other students who rode with us, but I had never seen about two-thirds of the other students who were on our bus. But again, I never had a hard time adapting to the environment or ever had to deal with any bullying or racism in the years I attended there. The only thing I remember was that these kids called themselves "The Greasers," who would go around bullying other kids, but for some reason, they never bothered me. I remember bringing The Greasers up to a friend of mine a couple of years ago while we were at a party and asking him why they never messed with me, and his response was, "Well, because you were much bigger than they were, and they were afraid of you." The Greasers were kids who tried to intimidate those they knew wouldn't fight back. One day, to see how they would react, I made it my purpose to go and walk right past them to see if they would say or try to do something to me. I had noticed them all hanging out in front of a store in our neighborhood. Before that moment, they had been picking on some kids I hung around with. As I walked past them and into the store, one of them nodded and said, "What's up?" I just kept walking. I did that to prove a point. They were the bullies, but at the same time, they always knew who to pick on. I was ready for whatever they were going to bring that day. I had no fear. They knew right away I was not the guy they wanted to mess with because nothing would go their way. Part of it may have been because they knew I was a star athlete and in good shape. I assumed they could see it in my face that I didn't fear them. After that, they never bothered any of my friends again. While at William Wirt, my gym teachers, Mr. Waunslat and Mr. Tucci, were excellent mentors for me. They always advised me and ensured that I stayed on a positive path. Mr. Waunslat, my basketball coach, encouraged me to play soccer because he said it would help me keep in shape. I had never played soccer before, so I figured, why not give it a shot? But that was short-lived. I went and played, but I wouldn't say I liked it because I didn't know what the hell I was doing out there. I was always offside, running around in circles, not knowing what to do. I was just lost out there. The game was much more complicated than I ever expected it to be. So, after playing for one season, I never played soccer again. That was the last time I ever played another sport besides basketball. We had two reasonably good basketball seasons during my 7th and 8th grades.

One of my best memories playing basketball at William Wirt occurred during one of my games during my final season in the 9th grade. We were playing against Laurel Junior High, and I was on fire. I ended up scoring 41 out of the 61 points. One of the things I was known for was my jumping abilities, and I was a big-time dunker. I was close to 6 feet, and even though I could score many points, no one else who was my size was dunking the ball like me. We ended up having a better season and winning the championship that year. I was also named Athlete of the Year. My junior high years were average overall. Although we only won one championship, I had a great time at William Wirt. Before graduating, I will never forget when Mr. Waunslat came over to me and said, "I can probably get in trouble for this, but I believe everyone expects a kid of your talent to go to public school because you're in the public school system." Before ending our conversation, he recommended that I go and look at DeMatha High School, a famous Catholic school not too far from William Wirt. Before this moment, I hadn't thought about DeMatha. Nor had anyone else brought it up to me. Once I graduated from junior high, I began focusing on basketball and looking forward to moving on to the next phase in my life. Back then, there was no AAU league like you see today. So, after my basketball season ended, I would play pickup games around the neighborhood, or I would go to different recreation centers like Glenarden Rec, Seat Pleasant, where Superstar NBA Great Kevin Durant played, or down to Palmer Park, where Gold Medalist and Middleweight Boxing Champion Sugar Ray Leonard used to train. Prince George's County is known for having many great athletes. I learned a lot from going to those gyms because many college ball players and older guys would come down and play against us. Larry Coleman, who played for the Globetrotters, was a good friend I would always play with. He and I would go around to other gyms looking for better competition to play against. Playing at recreation centers was big for us back then because it was a place where kids from all over the neighborhoods could go down and play. It was a place where I honed all my skills. I even had the opportunity to go to New York and play at Rucker Park under Mr. Cash, one of the other coaches in the recreation department. There wasn't a single day when I wasn't training to play basketball. I was on a mission to become the best basketball player I could be.

Chapter 5

Decision Time

Not too far from where we lived was Ms. Pat Osborne, who was originally from Boston. Her son John and I had played together at the Boys and Girls Club for many years and became best friends. I would often go over to their house to play basketball with him. Ms. Osborne knew how good of a basketball player I was, and even though she knew I had a bit of a crazy temper and needed some discipline, she saw something in me. She came up with the idea to come to our house to talk with my parents and convince them to enroll me at DeMatha. That was the second time I heard someone mention that I should go to DeMatha. Ms. Osborne had registered her son John at DeMatha and felt I had an opportunity to play basketball there. As they talked about it, my parents were very skeptical about sending me to a Catholic school. Plus, the other issue was that if I went to DeMatha, it meant that my parents now had to pay tuition. Back then, it was uncommon for kids in my neighborhood to attend private schools requiring tuition. Long story short, whatever she said to my parents, it worked. Ms. Osborne had sealed the deal for me to go to DeMatha. By taking an interest in me and my life, Ms. Osborne probably changed my entire life. I will never forget that and try to do the same for others through my foundation.

Pat Osborne

I remember finding out that my parents had both agreed for me to go to DeMatha. While at the dinner table with my younger brother and sister, my parents gave us a little speech, and then I heard them say, "Dereck, after talking to Ms. Osborne, we have decided to enroll you at DeMatha High School." I was ecstatic, thankful, and appreciative, and I promised my parents I would not disappoint them. At the time, I didn't know how big of a decision it was for my parents to make. It was a huge financial decision. It may not seem like it today, but paying a hundred and fifty dollars a year for me to go to school back then was a lot of money, not to mention they had two other kids to raise. Going to DeMatha was a big deal for me because you had to be an excellent student and an outstanding athlete to enroll there. I was also aware that nothing was guaranteed for me to play just because I was attending DeMatha. I also had to do my schoolwork.

After my parents decided that I was going to be attending DeMatha, I became aware that Coach Wootten, the DeMatha Coach, was hosting a very famous basketball camp at St John's High School in DC, which is where I met him for the very first time. All of the players from DeMatha would go down there to work the camp and make a few dollars. It was a good way for me to get to know some of the other players before entering our basketball season. After camp, we would play pickup games. It was like an audition to show the coaches how good we were. But aside from seeing me play, they also witnessed how hot-tempered I was. I remember getting in trouble and being pulled to the side by one of the coaches who tried to calm me down. I was very competitive and a bully on the court. I knew that going to DeMatha was going to change me. It was different from going to public school, where you had the privilege of wearing whatever you chose. At DeMatha, we had to wear slacks, a blue blazer, and a tie. Not abiding by the dress code also came with some consequences, so the strict environment changed my behavior naturally. I knew I had to act right if I wanted to play. Between that and all the other lessons I had learned along the way, it taught me that if I wanted to play there, I had to learn to behave myself. There was no more of me trying to chase players around to try and beat them up, trash-talking and getting into a fight over it or cursing at coaches and sitting on the bench for it. I had to get my anger under control and listen as much as possible. I focused heavily on being a good student and a disciplined basketball player who was now preparing to play for one of the country's greatest and most legendary high school coaches and Hall of Famer, Coach Morgan Wootten.

Chapter 6

Choose Wisely

The year was 1977. I can still remember feeling when I first walked into DeMatha High School. It was different in many ways from any other school I had attended because it was not only a Catholic School but also an all-boys school. When I first walked into the school, I only remember seeing many new kids I had never met. John Osborne was the only person I knew, which made me feel comfortable knowing at least one person.

I was very excited to be at DeMatha for many reasons. DeMatha was one of the most successful high school programs in the area and the country. Many great players went to DeMatha. There was Adrian Dantley, who played at Notre Dame and later became a 6-time NBA All-Star and two-time scoring champion while playing for several teams, including the Detroit Pistons, Los Angeles Lakers, and Utah Jazz, Kenny Carr, who went to NC State and played in the NBA for the Portland Trailblazers, Los Angeles Lakers, and the Cleveland Cavaliers. Another great legend who went to DeMatha was James Brown, who turned down every major school in the country to go to Harvard after graduating, which was unheard of then. James Brown later became a great sportscaster on the James Brown Show, The NFL Today on CBS, Fox NFL Sunday Pregame Show, and a Special Correspondent for CBS News.

James Brown

The school had a great history of having so many star players who went to prestigious schools after graduating, and now I am a part of that tradition. Everyone knew that if you went to DeMatha, you would eventually get a college scholarship, which was huge back then. For the past 42 years, every senior has earned a scholarship. Going to DeMatha wasn't just great news for my family and me. It made all my former coaches very proud of me, too. It was a big deal because I was the only kid from the Glenarden area who went to a school of that magnitude. Although everyone was happy, there was also some skepticism about me succeeding at DeMatha. I was going to face a lot of competition and play against some of the best players in our area.

Sophomore Year at DeMatha

One of the first guys I met at the school was Sidney Lowe. He was recognized as one of the best junior high school players from the DC area, while I was considered one of the best junior high players from the Maryland area. From day one, they always had us playing together on the same team during pickup games. We went on to play together as teammates for many years to come. Getting two of the best players in the area to play together was a huge deal. He and I would become teammates and develop a great relationship from day one. We not only got along well, but we also understood each other as basketball players. Before the beginning of our basketball season, Coach Wootten would always check on how all the ball players were doing. To try and get to know him better, I would often meet with him in his office and have conversations. During one of my first conversations with Coach Wootten, I learned there had been a scout from DeMatha who had attended my game against Laurel Junior High School, where I had scored 41 points. He told me that the scout was so impressed with how I played that he had gone back and expressed to him that a player at William Wirt Junior High went by the nickname Tweety that he needed to try and recruit. I didn't know a scout was there watching me play; it just happened that I had played so well at the right time. That was the game that had made them take a closer look at me. I want to share that because, as a player, you never know who's out there in the crowd watching you play.

Coach Wootten was a great friend of the legendary Head Coach of the Boston Celtics, Red Auerbach, who would often come down to watch some of our practices. Although I was never one of his students, Coach Wootten was also a history teacher at our school. When Coach Wootten and I spoke, he told me I might not be one of his starters; if most players heard that from their coach, they would transfer to another school the next day. But I trusted him. Knowing his history and how much he had accomplished helped me understand and accept whatever plans he had for all of us as his players. I knew that if I had attended my original high school, which would have been Duval High School, I would have been an automatic star player starting on the varsity team.

I will never forget when I first heard one of Coach Wootten's speeches to the team. He taught us one of the most important lessons: "It's not whether you start; it's whether you finish the game that matters most." I learned and accepted that quickly because it was a privilege and an excellent opportunity for me to play for a coach like Morgan Wootten at one of the best high schools in the country. I wanted to ensure that I set an excellent example for the team by always doing all the right things and being a leader. I wasn't into partying or feeling the need to go out and look for a girlfriend like the other kids in my neighborhood were. I just wanted to focus on basketball. That was it. I had always been a excellent student. I never had any issues with my grades or behavioral problems in the classroom. I was always interested in learning. However, before I go any further about DeMatha, I want to share a story that occurred during the school year and before our basketball season started. It was a moment that could have quickly gone wrong and where my dreams of becoming a basketball player could have soon disappeared. I need to share this situation because I know how easy it can be for kids to make the wrong decisions in their young lives, especially regarding money and peer pressure. This moment showed me that there were people out there who not only cared about me when it came to my future but also saw something in me and wanted to motivate and encourage me always to do better.

Around my neighborhood, there was a kid named Dwayne Nichols, his nickname was Space, who was also a good basketball player. He was strong, stood about 6'4, and weighed around 210 pounds with no fear. I had met him during my first year at DeMatha while playing a pickup game at the park. After one of our games, I got in his car and rode to his house to hang out. While in his room, I remember him reaching under his mattress and pulling out a stack of money. Now, before going to his house, I had no idea that he was into dealing drugs. I remember telling him, "Give me some of that money." Without hesitation, he responded, "No, I don't want you getting involved in any of this; you're just going to play ball." After realizing that Space was out there selling drugs, I should have made the right decision and never hung out with him again because I didn't want to get in any trouble. But I continued hanging out with him because I felt he was a cool kid and a basketball player.

About a week later, Space had come to pick me up after school so we could go and play ball. Suddenly, while driving towards the park, he happens to see this guy who owes him some money. Space yelled from his window, asking, "Hey man, you got my money?" Before the guy could even give him an answer, Space stopped the car right there in the middle of the street, grabbed his gun from his waist, and with his left hand, he just began pistol, whipping him over his head with the butt of his gun. While pounding him over his head, I could hear Space saying, "Where's my money at?" you better come up with my money." I was sitting there in the car saying to myself, "Oh my God, please don't let him kill this guy." I wanted to escape the situation quickly and never ride with him again. Those were probably the longest 45 seconds of my life.

My parents had always warned me to be careful about the kids I chose to hang out with, and it was at that moment I realized why. When Space got through with the guy, I saw blood everywhere. There I was in my gray slacks, a blue blazer, and my book bag, and I was out there hanging out with this gangster, acting crazy in broad daylight. Space finally got back in the car and drove away like it was nothing. I was sitting there speechless and scared to death. As tough as I was, I was now afraid of him. Without a single word said to each other, Space drove me to the front of my house and said, "I'll catch up with you later." We gave each other a fist pump, and I was out the door. It just wasn't a good look for me. Space could have killed the guy, or the police could have rolled up on us at any moment and arrested the two of us. Had any of those things occurred, you probably wouldn't be sitting there reading my story. That was the last time I hung out with Space because there was no telling what else would have happened. Although that situation with Space wasn't such a positive story, I still have to give him credit because he kept me away from getting involved in the drug game. He could have easily dragged me into the drug world, and I could have become a dealer just like him.

Unfortunately, when you play those games, there is a great chance it will eventually catch up to you. After spending many years of his life going in and out of prison, Space ended up murdered. It was unfortunate, but it was a positive that he kept me out of the drug world. Growing up in DC, many of us came across kids like Space and had those types of relationships, but it was a matter of whether you got caught up in that world. It all came down to the choices and decisions that you made. When I talk to kids these days, I always tell them that what you hang around is what you will become. Let me say this first: I am very thankful that Space cared enough for me, not just as an athlete but also to keep me away from the drug world. He could have easily said, "Ok, let's go and make some money," my entire life would have gone into an entirely different situation. Instead, he was honest and told me, "No." I am not saying I would have rather gone in that direction. What I am saying is this. When it comes to that world, it is very easy for young kids who don't have much and are so easily impressed with the money, the sneakers, the clothes, and the entire lifestyle. Many kids get involved because they believe nothing will ever happen to them. They see the money and nothing else. Especially if the guy you're next to has a lot of money—sort of like what happened to the late Len Bias. Len Bias was supposed to be the next great basketball star to come out of Maryland University and onto the NBA. Bias grew up right down the highway from me. He was from Prince George's County and attended Northwestern High School. Bias idolized me because I was one of the first Prince George's County players to attend DeMatha. Back then, he wasn't the Len Bias we later came to know as a star player at the University of Maryland; he grew as a player and was the most physical specimen I had ever seen wearing a basketball uniform. He had muscles everywhere and was very athletic. What happened to him is sad because if you compare all the great historical athletes who grew up in our area, Len Bias would have been an icon. I don't know much about anything he was doing off the court, but we later found out through the ESPN 30 for 30 "Without Bias" documentary that he was hanging around some pretty bad company the night he was drafted by the Boston Celtics. He was hanging out with a kid named Brian Tribble, who allegedly had provided Bias with pure, uncut cocaine. According to accounts, after Bias ingested the cocaine, Tribble had told him not to lean his head back because it would cause the drug to go straight to his head, which, of course, Bias did. He died of cocaine intoxication. Bias wasn't known to be a drug user or addict but choosing to hang out with the wrong company and celebrate with them ended up costing his life. I am telling this story because something similar could have happened if Space never told me he didn't want me to be a part of that world. I still remember the day Bias died. At the time, I was the assistant coach at George Mason, and I remember I was on my way to speak at a basketball camp at George Mason High School. I had heard the news over the radio, and I pulled off to the side of the road and cried like a baby. I couldn't believe it. I was numb. After that situation, I was sure I would never hang around anyone who would jeopardize my basketball career, life, and freedom. After that situation with Space, I made sure that I kept the promise that I had made to my parents when I told them I would never disappoint them, and I never saw Space ever again. I want to thank Dwayne "Space" Nichols for not allowing me to get involved in the business he was into because it might have saved my life.

Chapter 7

Becoming A Stag

Morgan Wootten was more than just a basketball coach. He taught us more about life than just the game of Basketball. He had sound principles about the game of Basketball, but to him, it was more about the process of playing the game and being part of a team. His philosophy was God first, Family second, Education third, and then Basketball. He taught us how to conduct ourselves and always ensured we wore a coat and tie when traveling.

He taught us how to be a great teammate and take constructive criticism. Those were the essential things that he would always emphasize to us. He would always take us on the stage after every practice and talk about life. Sometimes, it was giving us advice; other times, it was talking about his experiences or reading a poem. The significant thing about playing for him is that he showed us that he genuinely cared about us. He was just an excellent leader and very motivational. He was nothing like most coaches you see today who want to win at all costs and make everything about themselves. Morgan Wootten won 87 percent of all the games he coached. So, we always knew that to be successful, we had to follow his lead. He loved us as human beings, not just as basketball players. Of course, he wanted to win. But he also wanted us to become great people and win the game of life. That's one of the main things I will always cherish about him. Although recruited to play on the DeMatha varsity team, I had to try out; there was no question I would make the team. Could I have easily been one of the starters? Absolutely! But that wasn't the most important thing to us, and Coach Wootten made it very simple for us to understand that.

DeMATHA
"STAGS"
1977-78 BASKETBALL TEAM

COACH
PROVOST T. BURKE J. BRUEN M.WOOTTEN B. BARR M. BRUCE K. BROADDLUS B. MCGREGOR P. CLARK R. GROSS
C. BATES M. WHITLOCK J. CARROLL P. DEVITO P. WHITE C. BRANCH J. WASHINGTON C. GILDEA
M. HIBBS M. O'DRISCOLL D. MORLEY M. HOPSON A WASHINGTON S. LOWE D. WHITTENBURG K. EATON

In my first season, we ended with a 29-4 record while losing twice to St. John's in the regular season. St John's went on to win the championship that year. Although we didn't win it all, it was an excellent experience for me. I didn't start any games, but the best players always ended up on the court. I was often one of them. That system also taught me to be patient and wait my turn. Later that summer, the DeMatha High School team, and Howard University traveled together on a South America trip to participate in a tournament against international competition in Brazil, which was very different for me. That was the first time I had ever gone out of the country. Playing in Brazil was an excellent experience because we spent a lot of time together as teammates and learned how to play against the fiercest international competition. There was a bit of a struggle due to the language barrier, and we had to figure out how to navigate in a foreign country. We had to learn to speak a little Spanish to mingle with the local players or when we went out to eat together. It was a fun experience. We were in Brazil for 11 days and played about eight games where we went undefeated. My first year at DeMatha was a great learning process, and I couldn't wait to play again the following season.

DeMatha Stags
Picture from Sports Illustrated Magazine

In my junior year, we went undefeated, going 28-0. Only a few teams go undefeated. Being a part of that was special for us. We won Coach Wootten's first National Championship for DeMatha High School, which meant we were the country's Number 1 high school team. That was the first year they started acknowledging high school teams as National Champions. I was the second-leading scorer behind the late Tommie Branch, but I can't tell you what I averaged that year because it wasn't all that important to me. Ingrained in the DeMatha culture was that winning and being a great teammate was more important than individual statistics. Tommie Branch also had a brother, Adrian Branch, who was a high school All-American at DeMatha and then played at the University of Maryland before being drafted by the Chicago Bulls in the 1985 NBA draft. Although we had gone on a great run that year, the goal was never to go undefeated. It was still all about how we played the game. Going undefeated at DeMatha was not a big deal; winning was expected. We were in better shape than any of the teams we played against and blew away the competition. Most importantly, we were disciplined and were a strong team on the fundamentals. Our rivalries were Mackin and the defending champions, St. John's High School, but we dominated high school basketball for the next two years.

Coach Wootten's First National Championship

During my sophomore season, we played in the Raleigh Times Festival Tournament. Mike Brey, my former DeMatha teammate, later became a coach at Notre Dame and was also there playing at the tournament. During the time that we were there, we took the opportunity to visit Duke, North Carolina, and NC State. Mike Brey had gone along with us to take the tour, and I remember him turning around and looking at me and Sidney and saying, "You two little guys are going to end up right here playing at NC State together," and we just laughed at him. We also played in a tournament at the Baltimore Civic Center against Overbrook, and between games, we had a slam dunk contest. Two of my opponents for the slam dunk contest were Gene Banks, who was from West Philadelphia High School and ended up going to Duke University, and Albert King, who was from Fort Hamilton High School in Brooklyn, New York, who ended up at the University of Maryland. They were both promoted as the country's two best high school players. No one had any idea who I was back then, mainly because I wasn't even one of the starters on my team. All everyone saw was that there was this little, short guy from DeMatha who was outshining both. I ended up beating both in the slam dunk contest and being named the tournament MVP. That became my breakout party because it gained me more recognition.

After the season, I started to get a lot of letters from different colleges, but I needed something to stand out to me. In my senior year, college became prevalent, and I became more interested in figuring out where I would go. My last year at DeMatha was exceptional. Playing there gave me and my teammates the exposure we needed to get the attention of some of the big-time colleges. It's not like today, where everything seems backward, where the player's dream is to play in the NBA. Not that it wasn't our dream, but we all knew that our first step was college. It was also special to me because I was the first person in my immediate family to have the opportunity to attend a major college and receive a big-time scholarship. That wasn't just a big deal to me; it was also a big deal for my family. Although I was looking forward to college, I still had one more season to focus on. For the first time while playing at DeMatha, I was finally playing as a starter. Ten games into the season, I broke my fifth metatarsal bone, which was very painful. I couldn't believe that was happening to me in my very last year at DeMatha. I missed around 8 or 9 games, but I was able to come back and play the final few games of the season. We still managed to end the season 28-3 and beat Dunbar High School to win the City

Championship, played on the University of Maryland campus. After defeating Dunbar, we played in the Alhambra Catholic Invitational Tournament in Cumberland, Maryland, where all the top Catholic teams and other teams from the local area competed against each other. The big deal in the DC area was to make All Metropolitan, which I was chosen for even though I had missed several games. Once the season was over, I started the process of visiting colleges. I visited Rutgers, Penn State, and North Carolina State. Those were the only three colleges I visited. Because I had come up watching my cousin David Thompson play at NC State and loved Norm Sloan and his checkered sports jackets, North Carolina State was my first choice. It had always been my dream to play there and win the National Championship, just like they did in 1974. The visits were all great. My parents didn't get involved other than asking me how I felt about my visits. But other than that, they left everything up for me to decide. The people I confided in the most were Coach Wootten and my childhood friend and mentor, Guy Black because they knew more about sports and my opportunities. In my neighborhood, no one went to famous schools to play sports because they were afraid of being outshined and unable to get any playing time. I don't believe there were too many people in my neighborhood who knew about my notoriety at DeMatha or how good I was because it wasn't like I was playing at a school where I was averaging 30 points a game. I was in the newspaper all the time. DeMatha had a team concept about winning, not individual stats. I wasn't getting the notoriety that some of the other good players were getting at neighboring high schools because they were the team stars. There weren't any stars at DeMatha because we all played together as a team.

Chapter 8

Footsteps of My Idol

While in the process of trying to figure out what college I was going to attend, I had been chosen to play in the 1979 McDonald's Capital Classic game in DC. I played for the Washington DC All-Stars, and we went up against the USA All-Stars. Then, a week later, I played in the McDonald's All-American game in Charlotte. Not only did I hit the game-winning shot for the Washington DC All-Stars to beat the USA All-Stars, but I also hit the winning shot in the East versus West game. The Class of 1979 included players like Isaiah Thomas, James Worthy, Dominique Wilkins, Sam Bowie, and Ralph Sampson. That class was considered one of the best high school basketball classes ever. I remember hearing whispers in Charlotte that Dominique Wilkins, from Little Washington, North Carolina, was supposed to go to NC State with us. They were even saying he was going to be the next David Thompson. While we were practicing there in Charlotte, I remember going over to Wilkins's mother and saying to her, "Dominique is coming to NC State along with me and Sidney," and she says to me, "Dominique is not going to NC State; *he's going to Georgia.*"

The funny thing was that when I was visiting different colleges and trying to decide where I wanted to go, the University of Hawaii also invited me to go there on a tour. I told Coach Wootten I was considering going for the tour; he encouraged me not to go because he knew I wasn't interested in attending the University of Hawaii. And he was right because I just wanted to take advantage of a vacation to see Hawaii. The coach was still teaching me life lessons, and this one was about honesty. I still hadn't decided by this time, but my teammate Sidney Lowe had decided to go to NC State. Even though he and I always wanted to go to school together, we didn't have any dialogue about it. It would have been great if it worked out, but neither pressured the other into making any decisions.

The most significant thing for me was Monte Towe, who had also played with my cousin David Thompson on the 1974 National Championship team and was the assistant to Coach Sloan. Monte came by my house to take my brother Reggie and me to a Denver Nuggets game to see David Thompson play at the Capital Center. That was the first time I had ever watched my cousin play in person. I was so mesmerized by that. After the game, Monte stood around waiting for David to come from the locker because they had plans to hang out after the game. Once we were all in the car together, David asked me, "So, when will you finally decide where you're going?" I told him that I hadn't decided yet. My cousin turns to me and says, "Cuz, why don't you go ahead and get this over with." I knew what he meant by that, so I just said, "Okay," that's how I decided to go to NC State. I went on and signed the very next day. Sidney Lowe had already decided to attend NC State just a few days prior. Aside from wanting to follow in my cousin's footsteps, I chose to go to NC State for many other reasons. I loved Coach Sloan and the passion he had. The campus was so nice, and the people were kind, which also played a big part in why I chose to go there. Above all, I wanted to play in the ACC. Signing with a university wasn't as big of a deal as it is today, where they have press conferences and put on a hat to show where you chose to attend. My parents and I visited the university to sign my national letter of intent. Within a few days, I received a call from NCSU assistant coaches Marty Fletcher and Monte Towe. They congratulated me and expressed how happy they were I decided to go to NC State. My basketball career at DeMatha had ended, and my new journey playing at North Carolina State University was beginning. As it turned out, Mike Brey was right when he predicted that Sidney Lowe and I would play together as teammates in college, which was one of the best parts of my decision to go there. Sidney and I ended up being roommates at NC State. Aside from Sidney and me, we had another freshman named Thurl Bailey, who was 6'9 and from the DC area.

Sidney Lowe

I'll admit, as athletes, we did get treated a little more special than the average student, and I could sometimes see there was a little animosity towards us because we were at the training table on campus at the Case Athletic Center and eating different food from what the other students were eating. But I didn't have this elitist attitude; I felt I had a great experience mixing with the other students. I was a true student-athlete. Today, athletes don't hang around the campus anymore. They live in apartments; they go to class and are out of there. They don't mingle with other students or go to the student unions to play cards or pool. I used to go to the student union, hang out, and play spades all the time. One of my best friends, whom I used to play with all the time, was Tab Thacker, one of the actors in Police Academy. He was the first wrestling heavyweight champion at NC State. He was a great Spades player. He and I would hang out in the student center all day. But I know for sure athletes rarely do that these days. Things are just so much different nowadays. In fact, with the way things are today with technology, most kids rarely sit in a classroom. Their interaction with people could be much better. Back when I was in school, you had to go and meet with the teachers and walk around the campus just like the rest of the other students. I didn't have a car to get around in, so we just hung out and talked to each other. Today's star players lose a lot from not interacting with fellow students.

The only thing that felt odd was the stereotype that athletes weren't supposed to be in college. Most people felt that athletes only got accepted as special admissions or that we weren't smart enough to be there and only got in because of our athletic ability. I always told people that athletes earned their scholarships regardless of their opinions. We've spent many years playing on the playground, our parents taking us to practices and games where we developed our talent to become as good as we did. Therefore, it was a mutual deal. No one gave me anything I had to work hard to receive. It wasn't a handout. I earned it. The other stereotype was that every athlete from the inner city was poor or only had one parent. Later in my coaching years, those thoughts never crossed my mind regarding any athlete. I never cared whether the kids had one or two parents or if he came from the ghetto or a wealthy family. All that mattered to me was if they could play or not and if they were a good person.

As a student-athlete at NC State, I was excited and couldn't wait for basketball season to begin. I thought playing at DeMatha was a big deal, but I was now playing in front of a larger crowd. Not to mention that the rest of the country was now tuning in to watch us play. During my first year, I wore the number 4. However, the following season, until I graduated, I wore the number 25, which happened to be the same number Coach Towe used back when he played at NC State. My coach, Norm Sloan, had also played at NC State. Coach Sloan played for Everett Case, who brought basketball to the South and won the first five ACC Championships for NC State. Coach Sloan was a big part of the university's history, and his legacy is intact. As a coach, he was a competitive guy, and he hated North Carolina and wanted to win at all costs. He was very transparent and always told us the truth so we could trust him.

I remember the very first time I met Coach Sloan. He had come to pick us up so we could visit the campus at NC State, but before we did the visit, he took us out to dinner. In addition to being fiercely competitive, he wore these colorful checkered jackets that he became known for. I laugh to this day anytime that I tell this story about him. While on our way to the restaurant, Coach Sloan kept complaining about the speed bumps on the road. The funny thing was, he never slowed down when he went over them. He just continued going at whatever speed he was going and drove full speed right over them while muttering, "The hell with all these speed bumps; I don't give a crap about no darn speed bumps; I'm not going to keep letting them slow me down." I said to myself, "You know what? I'm going to play for this crazy coach". That was just the type of person Coach Sloan was. He wasn't going to let anything slow him down.

We had a pretty good team during my first year. We had a great player named Charles "Hawkeye" Whitney, who was from the DC area and had also played at DeMatha, so it made everything more comfortable for us all. The funny thing about Whitney was that he was assigned to be our host when we first visited NC State. But just minutes after meeting him for the tour, Sidney and I remember him turning to us and saying, "Listen guys, y'all just hang out here; I'll be right back," he just disappeared on us. We only saw him again the following year when we became teammates. But Hawkeye was a cool guy and a fierce competitor and was the leading scorer on our team that season.

Hawkeye was a big, powerful guy who was 6' 5, weighed about 245 pounds, and was my workout partner in the weight room. I will never forget the time he went up for a dunk against Georgia Tech, and one of the opposing players undercut him, causing Hawkeye to fall on his head, and he came up bleeding. Hawkeye came back up and started to rush toward the player who had fouled him, and my instinct was to grab Hawkeye and hold on to him until the rest of the team came over and helped me stop him. Hawkeye kept saying, "Let me go, I'm a kill this guy, let me go." Now, I wanted to hold onto him because I knew he would try to kill the Georgia Tech player, but also because we were winning the game, and if I had let him go, we would probably have lost. We ended up winning the game, and while we were in the locker room, Hawkeye came over to me and said, "Listen, you little jerk, don't you ever grab me like that ever again or I'm going to kill you." Everyone on the team was shocked that I had been able to hold him back from fighting. But the crazy thing was that when Hawkeye and I worked out together, he never changed the weights. He made me lift the same weight as him, eventually making me a stronger player. But there were no hard feelings between us. We just made a joke out of it and moved on.

We finished the season with an overall record of 20-8 and tied for second place in the ACC. In the ACC Tournament, we played Duke and lost in the first round. But our goal all year was to get to the NCAA Tournament and try to win the National Championship. Although Sidney, Thurl, and I were only freshmen, we had a good chance at competing against any team in the tournament. After being selected to play in the NCAA Tournament, we played against Iowa in the East Region in Greensboro, less than an hour from our campus. If we beat Iowa, we would have needed to win three more games to have a great chance of making it into the final four.

I remember we had been out there on the court doing our first warm-up and then headed back to the locker room. We were all in good spirits and felt we would beat Iowa. Unfortunately, once we had gotten back to the locker, Hawkeye Whitney came rushing in and announced to all of us that he had heard Coach Sloan would be leaving NC State and taking the job at the University of Florida. After being stunned by the news,

I noticed that our Assistant Coach, Monte Towe, was nowhere to be found, which I felt was odd. Towe not being there seemed to confirm that something terrible was going on. At the time, we were only aware that Coach Sloan and the Athletic Director disagreed.

There I was, playing for the university and coach I had always dreamed of playing for, in the tournament I had dreamed of playing in and finding myself perplexed. I remember saying, "I came here for Norm Sloan, and now he's leaving us; what will I do?" The weird part was that Coach Sloan was still there and had to coach us for the game against Iowa, but how seriously would he take the game? He was going around trying to tell us to go out and win the game, but in my mind, I was thinking, "What do you care? You're leaving us." We lost to Iowa, which eliminated us from the tournament. Coach Sloan was out of there as soon as the game was over. We should have beaten Iowa. But our team was just distraught. The next time I got to see Coach Sloan was at his funeral. It was unfortunate how things played out, but at the end of the day, I loved him as my coach. It wasn't until many years later that I found out why Coach Sloan allegedly decided to leave NC State to go and coach at the University of Florida. Coach Sloan, who had won the 1974 National Championship, had a year-to-year handshake agreement with Athletic Director Willis Casey. Coach Sloan found out that North Carolina Head Coach Dean Smith, who hadn't won a National Championship then, had a 5-year contract at UNC and a contract with Converse. When Coach Sloan approached Willis Casey about negotiating a contract, Casey refused, and that's when Coach Sloan decided to move on.

When the season ended, I couldn't help but wonder who would come in and take over the head coach position. I was still committed to staying at NC State but was confused about what was happening. All we could do was sit around and wait to see who the university would choose. Soon after, we heard rumors that NC State had offered my former high school coach, Coach Morgan Wootten, the head coach position. I became excited to hear that, but there was no guarantee that he would accept the position. It would have been an excellent move for him to come and coach us at the university. I remember Sidney and I going as far as calling Coach Wootten at home to try to convince him to take the position. "You got to come, coach, please; we need you," I remember saying to him. But that never happened. Coach Wootten turned down the offer. I must admit I was crushed and disappointed about the whole incident. The only thing in our minds that summer was, "Who's going to coach us"? And then, straight out of central casting, comes Coach Jimmy Valvano.

Chapter 9

Jimmy V

Before I go into Coach Jimmy Valvano becoming our coach at NC State, let me tell you a funny story about how I had already met him before all of this. After my senior year at DeMatha, I played in an AAU tournament called The Boston Shootout. All these teams from the East Coast were playing in the tournament. We were playing against Red Bruin and his New York AAU team, and we went into triple overtime and won. After the game, Sidney and I were walking, and we both felt someone grab us by the back of our necks and say, "Hey, I'm Jim Valvano. I own a college, and I love the way you guys play, and I want you guys to come and play for me." Sidney and I just started laughing, and we just continued walking. Fast forward to the following year, when NC State was trying to find us a coach, Sidney and I sat down at the press conference, and Jim Valvano came in. I leaned over to Sidney and said, "That's the coach that came up to us in Boston and told us that he owned a college." Our assistant coach, Ed McClain, sitting close by, had overheard what I said to Sidney and told us, "Valvano coached at Iona College, he doesn't own a college." I had thought Coach Valvano owned a college the entire time.

Valvano, an Italian from New York who was not the conventional coach, must have done a hell of a sales job to convince Athletic Director Willis Casey because the two were the complete opposite. Judging by how we knew Casey, none of us would have ever thought he would have given someone like Valvano a shot. Valvano didn't seem like a coach; he seemed more like an entertainer. But there was something very magical about Jimmy Valvano that Casey saw. Valvano had such a great personality that it helped him understand how he presented himself during the interview. Coach Valvano had infectious enthusiasm, so I could understand how he likely blew away his competition for the job. You also have to remember that Dean Smith from North Carolina was an example of what a coach should be and look like. Valvano wasn't liked from the very start by most of the other coaches in the ACC because they felt he wasn't a traditional coach. I assume, in their eyes, Coach Valvano seemed a little cocky and was a slick talker. It was a code for calling him a Yankee. No one had ever seen a guy like him down in the ACC. But at the same time, Coach Mike Krzyzewski wasn't liked in many ways either. Coach K was a Polish guy from Chicago, and they were getting ready to fire him after three years at Army. Barry Jacobs said something interesting in his book "Across the Lines". He said those two guys were depicted and teased about being ethnic. People couldn't even pronounce the last name Krzyzewski correctly. The great thing was that both coaches were clever enough to defuse their differences by making jokes about it. Coach K would say things like "Yeah, yeah, I'm a Polack," and Coach Valvano would say something along the lines of "I know, I'm a Guinea," which was a great way to show that none of what they were saying was getting to them to the point where it would become a distraction to them. Humor is often the best remedy and works wonderfully to diffuse the issue of race.

The first time I heard Jimmy Valvano mentioned as our coach, I had no idea what to think. I was happy that we had finally found a coach, but we didn't know what to expect because of who he was and how he looked.

I will never forget Coach Valvano's first statement in our first practice. He said, "I came here to win a National Championship." He said, "I'm going to look at you as a person, student, and player." From day one, he made it a point to let us know that his office door was always open if we wanted to talk to him at any time. That was so impactful because it was similar to Coach Wootten's philosophy at DeMatha. Hearing those types of things made us feel confident that Coach Valvano was there because not only did he want to win the championship, but he also cared about us. Remember, Sidney and I had only lost seven games at DeMatha. We were used to winning. So, there was no pressure on us when Coach Valvano mentioned his goal was winning the national championship. Once he had expressed that it was his dream, nothing would get in his way of winning it. He was precisely the type of coach we needed.

The first time Coach Valvano entered the gym, he sat us all in a circle and told us about his dream of winning the national championship. After a few practices, he began having us cut down the net. There were no drills and no balls on the court. It was us, Coach Valvano, and a pair of scissors. We would climb on each other's shoulders and cut the net down one by one. The coach would cut the last piece of the net down, and we would celebrate like it was the real thing. We all thought he was crazy! It felt a little weird at first, but after doing it a couple more times, the more he engraved it in our thoughts, the more we believed in it. It was enjoyable. It was all about creating the vision in our minds. He said later in his famous ESPY speech that what was most important to him in life were three things: where you started, where you were, and where you were going. Coach Valvano had us rehearsing for the place where he was taking us.

Our goals from day one was three-pronged. We wanted to be first-generation graduates, win the national championship, and then go to the NBA. It's not like today, where it's the complete opposite. Kids want to go to college and the NBA, and "yeah, ok, we'll take a degree too." The idea of going to college has a different meaning and effect than it did when I was growing up. Today, some student-athletes see it as a road to the NBA. They have it backward. Reminding college athletes that 99% will not end up in the NBA or NFL or become entertainers or singers is important because It's not easy. Pursuing a dream is part of a journey that might go in your favor, but if it doesn't, you also must prepare to succeed in something else in case it all fails. Plus, even if you do make it to the NBA, you have to know how to manage your money, and your life will be enriched by having an education.

As the adults in these young kids' lives, we must take on the responsibility of making them aware of those situations. Coaches like Morgan Wootten and Jimmy Valvano were always there to constantly remind us of that. Our team felt lost when Coach Sloan left us. We were all shocked about it. Then, when Coach Wootten didn't accept the offer for the coaching position, that was a huge disappointment because we at least knew who he was; we knew his history. But when Jimmy Valvano became our coach, we felt it would be extraordinary from the beginning. He was just the type to make you feel that way.

In our first season under Coach Jimmy V in 1980, we went 14-13 overall. It was a disappointing start. I don't feel it had anything to do with his coaching; we didn't have a good season. Transitioning to a new coach and new system can take time. We liked him and his coaching style, but we couldn't win. During my first year under Coach Sloan, I got a lot of playing time. During my sophomore year, Coach Valvano approached me at one of our practices and said, "Listen, for us to be a stronger team, we need to have Kenny Mathews start and have you come off the bench. Would you mind doing that for the team? "Kenny Mathews was a senior and from the DC area. Without hesitation, I told him, "Coach, whatever you feel we need to do to strengthen the team, I'm in." I wasn't disgruntled or even upset about it because I knew I would get enough playing time whether I started or not. When Coach Valvano first took over as our coach, he came to me and mentioned that he had heard I was a terrific scorer and would let me take around 15 shots, and I had to give him at least 18 points in return. I said, "Coach, just give me the green light, and I will give you 20 a game". That shows you the type of relationship he had with his players. He was very upfront and candid with us. That's why we embraced him the way we did.

Jimmy Valvano was just a player's coach. He was the type who understood and sought the advice of the players. He gave the players ownership of the team. We would be in the huddle, and he would ask us, "What do you guys think? Should we play man or zone? What do you guys see?" He wasn't the type of coach to say things like, "I'm the coach; you do what I tell you to do." He would even go on the court with us and shoot during drills. Most coaches didn't do that. He was the epitome of a player's type of coach. Having been a good player at Rutgers himself, we felt comfortable with him. Coach Norm Sloan, who recruited us, had played for Everett Case at NC State and had a different personality. He was tough and wouldn't hesitate to curse you out to the point where you felt you had no choice but to respect him. He may have cared about us, but he didn't have that open-door policy where you could go in and talk to him about your problems. Coach Valvano was the complete opposite. He would teach us that practice was supposed to be fun. He had a very different style than the conventional type of coach.

So, when he asked if I minded coming off the bench, it wasn't even a problem. It wasn't that big a deal because that was the DeMatha training under Coach Wootten, where he would always tell us that "it's not important if you start, it's important that you finish the game." I was already used to it. Again, if you tell any player today, they will probably leave the program. I give credit to my upbringing; all my success and the basis of who I became is due to the groundwork my parents, teachers, and coaches instilled in me. They shaped my character. Trusting and believing in them led me on the right path. It wasn't so much that I was only learning from what they all said, I knew much more from what I saw and how they conducted themselves. I had great role models.

When people approach me, they always ask me how I became such a workaholic. I always tell them it is because I saw my parents working hard to provide for us. I learned through my journey that transparency plus truth equals trust. That was the most significant thing I learned from my mentors, teachers, and coaches. They were all very transparent and truthful with me; therefore, I realized I could trust them. In today's culture, there's little transparency and little truth; accordingly, there is little trust in what anyone says. Sports are very transparent and truthful; therefore, you can trust what you see because it is what it is. You can't make it political; you must play to win. You can't show favoritism because it will show up if you do. Sports is what it is. No matter your color, where you came from, or how great you are, you must trust your coach and set aside your thoughts regardless of how you feel.

I trusted Coach Valvano to make the best decisions because I knew he also wanted to win. Coach Valvano came in from day one, sharing his dream of winning the national championship. I had to trust him as the coach, respect his views, and allow him to lead the way. Sometimes, I would go to his office after class, and we would sit there and have many conversations about other things besides basketball. Some were funny, and some were about the things happening across the country and worldwide. There was one conversation that we had that I will never forget. It was about racism. Although I knew that racism existed, I had never dealt with any significant incident personally.

Now, remember that Coach Valvano was just an Italian from New York; he was not the unanimous choice for the coaching position. There weren't many people who felt NC State should have hired him, and to be one hundred percent truthful, him having an all-Black starting 5 wasn't even something I had ever thought about. When I began working on documentaries, I became more aware of the significance of those types of things. So many things go on behind the scenes that the public never knows what we, as players and coaches, deal with. Yes, winning is very important to all of us. But at the end of the day, it's also about having fun.

There should never be any reason why anyone who plays sports or is in some entertainment business should ever deal with any form of hate or discrimination. I will never forget the day Coach Valvano pulled out one of the letters he had received, which said, "I can't believe you're going to start an all-Black starting 5." Coach Valvano would often receive those types of letters. He would never allow any of those things to get under his skin or bother him to the point where they would affect his coaching in any way. Instead, he would use whatever he could to teach us a lesson about life. After reading the letter, he said, "This is why you have to get your education because one day, you're not going be a basketball player, and you may have to find another way to become successful." I didn't know if people treated him that way because we didn't win it all or because they didn't like him. We never lost hope. We had a great team and started looking forward to the next season. There was not a player on our team that didn't like coach Valvano. That year just allowed us to feel things out, and we got to see his coaching style. It was also Valvano's first year coaching in the ACC, so it was also a learning process for him.

During the spring before the 81-82 season in my junior year, I hosted many of the recruits who visited our school. One of them was Michael Jordan, who came onto our campus for a tour. I had never heard anything about Jordan before meeting him because you must remember, he played varsity in his senior year at Emsley A. Laney High School. He was very athletic and a good player but was far from the superstar he became when he got to the NBA. He had a lot of potential, and most of the time, schools usually go out recruiting certain players because they hear other schools are going after them. The University of North Carolina, our fierce rival, was recruiting him hard, so we tried everything to get him to come to us. From my recollection, he had already visited the University of North Carolina.

When he arrived for his visit, I treated him like any other player. He came with his parents and a couple of his brothers. I took Jordan out and showed him a good time, but he was quiet and uninterested. Now, remember, David Thompson was his idol, and he and his family grew up admiring David, who played at NC State. After spending a couple of hours with any recruit, I would have a sense if they were interested judging by how the visit went and their reaction. His family seemed to have had a great time during the visit, but I immediately knew his thoughts were elsewhere. He was quiet and wasn't all that confident yet. After the visit, I told Coach Valvano not to expect Jordan to come to our school, and that was it.

In my junior season, the goal was the same as the previous year: to win the National Championship. Valvano talked to us about how we needed to break down the season into four parts. First, the regular season, where the goal was to win at least 20 games, then play in the ACC tournament, get into the NCAA Tournament, and finally, win the national championship. We had our full-time starters in Sidney Lowe, Thurl Bailey, and me. As a team, we had a little more experience as juniors and believed we had a good enough team to win it all. We went into the season ranked 20th in the nation. We bounced back from the year before and had a good season with a 22-12 record.

We got a good draw for the NCAA Tournament and felt we had a great chance to advance; in the end, things didn't go our way. We played against East Tennessee Chattanooga, with Dominique Wilkins' brother Gerald on their team. We lost to them in the first round, which was very disappointing. We had a better team, but we didn't play well. We felt pressure to win because we lost in the first round, and our rival, the University of North Carolina Tar Heels, won the 1982 National Championship. That's the game where that timid recruit Michael Jordan hits the shot in the corner to seal the win as a freshman. Our fans had to hear about that all year, and it also put a lot of pressure on Coach Valvano.

Chapter 10

Miracle Season

Coach Valvano always told us, "When it comes to college, the experience goes very quickly, and opportunity has a window, so take advantage of it now because before you know it, your college career is over." Sort of like the message Coach John Thompson was trying to deliver with the flattened basketball on his desk I had mentioned at the beginning of my story. When it comes to college sports, or any sports for that matter, athletes and coaches are constantly judged by wins and losses. No one cares about how good you are or how impressive your numbers are at the end of the season. Everything boils down to winning the championship, cutting the nets, and putting the banner up.

Front Row, (l-r) Alvin Battle, Thurl Bailey, Sidney Lowe, Dereck Whittenburg, Quinton Leonard, Harold Thompson. Middle Row: George McClain, Walt Densmore, Walter Proctor, Cozell McQueen, Lorenzo Charles, Mike Warren, Terry Gannon, Ernie Myers. Back row: Head trainer Craig Sink, manager Gary Bryant, assistant coach Ed McLean, assistant coach Ray Martin, head coach Jim Valvano, assistant coach Tom Abatemarco, assistant coach Max Perry, manager Steve Whitt, assistant trainer Jim Rehbock.

1982-1983 N.C. STATE ROSTER

It was now my senior year at NC State and my last chance to win it all. We entered the season ranked in the top 25 in the polls. Like the two prior seasons, we went into the season by following the same script. There was nothing different about it besides that it was now my final year. I went into the season with three goals. I wanted to win it all, graduate college, and get drafted by a team in the NBA. I also asked Coach Valvano if the team could wear "Shell Toe" Adidas sneakers. I asked because I thought they made you a great basketball player when you stepped on the court. Stay with me; I'll explain how that theory came about.

In my younger days, most players wore Chuck Taylors on the court. But if you had on Adidas, not only would it have been considered cool to have them, but it also meant that you were a pretty good basketball player. I remember being a kid playing a pickup game with a few of my friends at one of our local parks; this had to be in the summer of 1976, and right before I started at DeMatha, Sugar Ray Leonard had just won the Olympic Gold Medal in boxing. I was out there wearing my Chuck Taylors like I always did. On the court, I saw a guy named Janks Morton, who happened to be one of Sugar Ray Leonard's trainers. Janks, a strong guy and a pretty good basketball player, also used to come out and play with us occasionally.

He was wearing Shell Toe Adidas. I remember saying to Janks, "Hey man, I like those shoes." I was only trying to compliment him on his shoes, that was all. He then turns to me and says, "For you, young fella, I'm going to do you a favor; what size do you wear?" After telling him I wore a size 12, he said, "Perfect, take these because I know you're going places in life." He gave me his shoes, and he took mine. I couldn't believe it. You have no idea what that meant to me. I wore those shoes every day after that. It was just the most incredible thing; I mention Janks because, like my old friend Space, he was also one who just believed in me. So, my reason for asking Coach Valvano if we could wear Adidas was to look cool as a team out there on the court, but it was also my way of thanking Janks for doing what he did for me. That was around the time when Nike had just come out. At the time, Coach Valvano was under contract with Nike, so a certain percentage of the players on our team had to wear their shoes. Coach allowed only the seniors, Sidney Lowe, Thurl Bailey, and me, to wear the Adidas shoes. But most importantly, we had just one more opportunity to go out there and win it all.

Remember, Sidney Lowe and I had been playing together since high school and had only lost seven games in high school. We had been used to winning. Our mindset was that if we followed the process, we would always win. The big difference was we were now playing in the toughest conference in college. Not to mention that the three-time player of the year and best player in the country, Ralph Sampson, was in our league. Plus, other premier and future first-round NBA players like Michael Jordan (UNC), Sam Perkins (UNC), Larry Nance (Clemson), and Len Bias (Maryland) played in our conference. It was challenging when it came to trying to win the ACC tournament, let alone the National Championship. Things back then were nothing like today, where players leave after playing one season and declare they are entering the NBA draft. We had to play against almost every star player all four years. Take, for example, Ralph Sampson. Some NBA teams tried to go after him since his first year, but he loved playing at Virginia so much that he decided to stay in school. He knew he was going to make it to the NBA eventually. He also knew how important it was to get his degree.

We had a pretty good team going into my senior season, but we didn't have an A-list guy. Sidney and I were experiencing notoriety because we played at an influential high school. But regardless of all the players I mentioned, Coach Valvano continued having us cut down the net during practice to engrave it in our heads that the goal was to put the championship banner up. We started the season playing very well. We were in the national spotlight and viewed as an incredible team. We knew we had some challenging games coming up that wouldn't be easy to win, but we truly felt we had what it took to go up against any team we faced. The fact that we hadn't beaten Ralph Sampson in 7 straight tries, and Virginia was ranked number 2 in the nation, gave us even more motivation to want to beat

Virginia. We were ranked 19th. When it was time to play them again, our record was 8-2. That game was our second conference game, which was going to be live on national television, and we knew they would come out strong, but we had no fear. We knew from the moment we stepped out on that court that it would be a battle. Our goal was to win the national championship regardless of who was playing against us on the court. And what a battle it was. Unfortunately, no one expected it to go the way it did.

They had just implemented the three-point line that year, 17 feet 9 inches from the basket, and we were a good shooting team. All my points in that game against Virginia were from behind the three-point line. I had made seven three-pointers and had 27 points by halftime. We were up 14 points going into the locker room. I was on fire that day. We all felt like we would finally beat the great Ralph Sampson. We come out for the second half, and while taking a jump shot in the corner, I come down and land on Othell Wilson's foot. I felt the pain. I remember getting up from the floor and telling myself to try and walk it off. I would try and do everything in my power to stay out there. In my mind, nothing would get me off that court without first beating Ralph Sampson. When I saw our trainer, Jim Rehbock, coming out to check on me, I told him not to come on the floor because I felt I would be alright. But that wasn't the case. Just like I had done in high school during my senior year, I ended up with the same injury in my senior year in college, only this time it was the opposite foot that I had broken. It didn't seem like it at first, but it was a painful injury.

Jim Rhebock & Coach Valvano helping me off court.

I remember returning to the bench and noticing Coach Valvano kept looking down to see if I would get up and return to the court. I could see it all over his face that he worried about not having me out there. I will never forget going into our locker room and hearing the doctor tell me that I would be out for 6 to 8 weeks. When Coach Valvano heard him say that, he banged his hand on the door and walked out in disgust. Now, you have to remember, because I had been down this road before when I had broken my foot at DeMatha, I knew what I had to do to get back on the court. I wasn't as devastated as anyone else would have probably been because I never thought in my mind that I wouldn't get back on the court. My mindset was different.

The fans at Wolfpack Nation were heartbroken because one of the star players was out, and he might not come back. Everyone, including some of our players, felt our season was doomed. Virginia ended up coming back and beating us by 8 points. It was pivotal for North Carolina State University because we genuinely felt good enough to win that year. I ended up having to get a screw put in my fifth metatarsal to try and help it heal faster. The next day, Coach Valvano came up to me while I was sitting in his office and said, "You know what?" you're going to come back like Willis Reed did in the 7th game with the Knicks, and we're going to win the championship. The same way he always did when he had us cutting down the net, he had me visualizing getting back on the court. Of course, I didn't know it would happen, but it was like, "Wow, coach really feels I was going to come back." It was almost like he could look into the future. I wanted to do everything I could to get back on the court.

Just three days after my injury, I arrived at Reynolds Coliseum with one of my coaches, we went through the back doors to watch one of our home games. As I was walking through, they asked me for my ticket. I remember saying to myself, "A ticket?" That situation brought me back to the conversation Coach Valvano and I had when he said to me, "They will soon forget you, and that's why you have to get your education." It was an eye-opening moment for me because not only had Coach and I talked about it, but I was also one of the star players on the team. The ticket-taker had no idea who I was. Had it not been for assistant coach Ed McLean, she would not have allowed me to go in to watch my own game. I always remember to tell students, especially the star athletes, the story of how soon they forget about you.

The beauty of that period was just how Coach Valvano held steady and showed tremendous leadership and resolve. He did a great job keeping everyone's spirits up and feeling hopeful.

While sidelined, I was the team's biggest cheerleader. I was there at every game, cheering everyone on. I recall that when we played the University of North Carolina, our last regular season game at home, who we hadn't beaten since my first year. Right before the game, I hobbled onto the court on my crutches to take a few shots. I made most of them. I remember telling Sydney Lowe he needed to be aggressive and take more shots. We ended up beating UNC, which boosted our confidence. During this time, Ernie Myers had taken over my spot. As a team, we didn't do too well, and we went on a bit of a slide. I knew I had to do whatever it took to get back out there to help the team win.

About three weeks later, the doctor came and looked at my X-ray, told me that my foot was about 75 to 80% healed, and asked me how I felt. It was still a little painful then, but I told him, "I'm ready to play." I remember returning for my first practice, and we were having a scrimmage game. The coach put me on the second team, and I was trying to fight my way back to the first team. I came back, meaning business, and my second team beat the first team. I was very excited and felt good. Then, Coach Valvano pulled me to the side and said, "Hey, Whitt, we adjusted to you coming back; now you have to adjust to us." It was such a timely and mental statement coming from him. I had realized that Ernie Myers had played well, Sidney had stepped up, George McClain and the rest of the team had adjusted and started to win. I had to insert myself back into the lineup by adapting to them. The other coaches said there was a dilemma before our next game because Myers had been playing great and was trying to figure out if they should put me on the starting lineup. In the end, Coach Valvano decided that because I was a senior, he would start me like nothing had ever happened, and we picked up from there.

When I came back, our next away game was against none other than the team I had broken my foot against earlier in the season, Ralph Sampson and the Virginia Cavaliers. I don't think they were expecting me to play that night. Guess what? I was ready. My first shot was a 25-foot swish, and I remember the crowd saying, "Oooh." It felt good getting back out there. Although we had a pretty good game, we lost. Then, we also lost my second game back to freshman Len Bias and the Maryland Terrapins. After losing to Maryland, I stormed into the locker room and gave my team the riot act as a source of motivation. Ultimately, I told the team, "This is our last chance; we have to step it up." We closed out the 82-83 regular season by demolishing Wake Forest 130-89 in our last home game and ended up with a record of 17-10.

Chapter 11

Destiny In the Making

Here's a piece of history that many people forget. At the time, we were still considered a bubble team and weren't sure if we would be selected to play in the NCAA Tournament. We didn't know if we could get in with being in 4th place in our conference. Coach Valvano reminded us that we needed to win some conference games or the ACC Tournament to get in. I know for sure that had I not broken my foot, there was no question that we would be locked in. We couldn't focus on just that; we had to focus on what was happening in the present and do whatever we had to do as a team to get in.

By now, we were headed to the ACC Tournament in Atlanta, and coincidentally, after recently beating Wake Forest, we had to play them again in the first round. That game was more challenging than our last game against them. Both teams played well. We were behind with a few minutes left; Sidney Lowe hit two free throws to tie the game. For some reason, Wake Forest stalled by passing the ball around, allowing the clock to run so they could take the last shot. Now, remember, there was no shot clock back then. Instead of continuing to allow them to run out the clock, Coach Valvano decided to call a timeout. After the timeout, we came out in a trapping defense. You could instantly tell that they weren't expecting that from us. As they attempted to make a pass, Sydney Lowe stole the ball and drove down the court on a 3-on-1. I thought he would pass the ball to me, but instead, he looked over and passed the ball to Lorenzo Charles.

As Charles attempted to make his shot, he was fouled, sending him to the free-throw line for two shots. There were only 3 seconds left in regulation; all he had to do was make one, and we could win the game. You could see the pressure on Charles' face when he missed the first free throw. But Lorenzo Charles then manages to make the second one. Wake Forest then takes out the ball and, in a desperate attempt, shoots from near half-court. The ball goes over the backboard, and we win the game 71-70. I don't know what made me do it, but I ran up to Coach Valvano, hugged him, and picked him up. We were all happy, but we still had a lot of work to do. Coach Valvano says, "Great job, but if we win the next one, we will probably get into the tournament." this was where the slogan Survive and Advance began.

Hugging Coach V

Our next game was against the defending champions, the University of North Carolina, in the semifinal game. I remember telling myself, I'm going to go in there and kick Michael Jordan's ass. I didn't consider him a great player because I thought I was better than him back then. Here's a fun fact for you. Most people never seem to remember that

I outscored Michael Jordan in every game we played against each other and even throughout our career in college.

Versus Michael Jordan (1983)

That day, I had a terrible game and did absolutely nothing during regulation. None of my shots were going in. Somehow, we just managed to stick around, and before you knew it, Jordan fouled out, and we ended up tying the game. UNC had a great chance to win the game. With just two seconds left, they inbounded the ball right in front of our bench and threw a pass across the court to Sam Perkins, who was all alone when he caught the pass right behind the three-point line. He turns around and shoots up a three-point attempt. As I'm watching the ball up in the air and sailing closer to the basket, I think, "It's over, no championship for us." Now, if you go back and watch the shot in slow motion, that ball touched the back of the rim, appeared to be heading through the net, and bounced right back out, and we went to overtime. We couldn't believe it. Had that shot gone in, you would probably be reading Sam Perkins's book instead of mine.

Although Jordan was on the bench, they still had Sam Perkins on the court, but we felt we had a great shot to win the game. UNC came out strong and went up 6 points with just two minutes left in overtime. All they had to do was hold the ball and run the clock down, and our season is over. We felt we had to do something. Again, this is where Coach Valvano was at his best. He comes up with a crazy strategy and tells us to foul to pressure them while attempting to make their free throws. At first, it seemed ridiculous to foul them because they were up six points. He was asking us to do what no coach would ever ask players to do while behind like that in the game.

Another critical point is that we could have kept fouling them because the rules weren't like today, where you go into the bonus and earn two shots. There was no shot clock then, so they could have easily just held on to the ball. But the strategy worked. We fouled them three times straight, and they missed all their free-throw attempts. In the meantime, we kept scoring and managed to cut the lead to 4, then we fouled them again. Suddenly, we begin to feel the momentum shifting our way. We put them on the line 3 times straight, and they missed three straight one-and-ones.

UNC guard Jim Braddock, an 86% free throw shooter, came down the court, and we fouled him to put him on the line to shoot a one-and-one. Under the intense pressure, Braddock misses his free throw. With only a minute left, we inbound the ball, and I went straight across the baseline and right under the basket to score on a layup. We go up one and take the lead for the first time in the game. From there, we never looked back. We ended up beating UNC 91-84, and we moved on to play none other than Ralph Sampson and the Virginia Cavaliers in the ACC Championship game. After winning the game against the UNC, I ran up to Coach Valvano again, hugged him, picked him up, and said, "We won another one for you." He says, "If you win the next game, you're definitely in." From that game on, hugging Coach Valvano after winning a game became a ritual.

When it came to facing Virginia who were the number one team in the country at the time, no one thought we would be able to beat them. And judging by the way they came out to play, you could tell they were coming to try to destroy us. Ralph Sampson dunked on our whole team three or four times in a row. In fact, *Dick Vitale, who was the commentator for ESPN at the time, was there providing analysis of the game,* and even he didn't believe we could beat Virginia. Sampson was dominating us. Within minutes, they were up by 8 points, and Coach Valvano called for a timeout. During the timeout, Coach scrapped the game plan we had and came up with a new strategy. The strategy was to double team Ralph Sampson the rest of the game while the other three played zone. That changed everything for Virginia. Once we were able to slow down Sampson from scoring, we managed to keep the game close all the way to the very end. Coach Valvano had once again played a winning chess move. With just 40 seconds left in regulation, Sampson got a pass down in the paint, and you can see he thought he had an open lane to dunk the ball. Right next to the 7 foot 4 Sampson was our 6 '1 guard Terry Gannon, who somehow managed to stick his hand in and strip the ball out of his hands as he was going up for the dunk. Any other time, Sampson would have dunked that ball over any player who would have gotten in his way. Gannon's only play was to do something before Sampson left the ground. After stripping the ball, Gannon passed the ball downcourt, and we managed to run out the clock to win the ACC Conference Championship game 81-78. We had finally beaten Virginia. When the game was over, I looked for Coach Valvano, ran up to him, and gave him his hug. It felt good cutting down the net after practicing from the moment Coach Valvano took over as our head coach. Not that I ever had any doubts; the dream Coach V had always shared with us was now starting to become a reality where you could feel it. We remembered what Coach Valvano said after the Wake Forest game: "Survive and Advance, one game at a time.

Chapter 12

Cardiac Pack

Since we had just won the ACC Tournament, we thought we would be playing somewhere on the East Coast. Instead, they shipped us out to Corvallis, Oregon, to play Pepperdine in the first round of the NCAA Tournament Western Regional Bracket. And who else was shipped out West with us? You guessed it, the University of Virginia. We couldn't get away from them. Pepperdine, led by the legendary coach Jim Harrick, had a good team. I believe that in their minds, they looked at us like we were a team they could beat; we felt the same way towards them. The funny thing was we were more concerned about the hotel they put us in than we were about playing them. If you ever watched the Survive and Advance documentary, you will see what I am talking about. Our hotel was just raggedy. As for the game, we were going at it, and it went into overtime. With a minute to go in overtime, Pepperdine was up by 6 points. It wasn't looking too good for us. Again, there was no shot clock, and the three-point shot was only allowed for regular-season play. It was not allowed during the tournament. Regardless of how many times we had been down and faced elimination, we always found a way to pressure our opponents to make them commit mistakes.

While inbounding the ball, Pepperdine threw up a lazy pass near halfcourt. Sidney Lowe cut across, stole the ball, then passed it to Lorenzo Charles for a quick basket and cut their lead down to 4 with 47 seconds left. Once Pepperdine inbounded the ball, we went to what had worked for us all along. We started fouling them and putting them on the line for the one-and-one free throws. Now, if you go back and watch the game, the commentator said, "Sidney Lowe, his career is over," as he walked toward the sideline after fouling out. That's how close we were to losing that game. With 30 seconds left in the game, Lowe had fouled Dane Suttle, who was not only Pepperdine's all-time leading scorer but also an 84% free throw shooter. As we look over to their bench, you can see them celebrating as if they had already counted us out. I could even hear one of their players talking trash to me.

Suttle then goes to the free-throw line and misses his shot. Lorenzo Charles grabbed the rebound with 26 seconds left on the clock, and we were down 59-55. He passes the ball to George McClain, who tosses a pass from halfcourt to Thurl Bailey, who dunks it in and brings us within 2 points. As Pepperdine inbounds the ball, we again had to foul Suttle. Suttle goes to the foul line to shoot the one-and-one and misses again. We knew right then and there that we had a psychological advantage. Their players were no longer trash-talking from the bench. You could tell they were very nervous. After Suttle's miss, Lorenzo Charles grabs the rebound and passes it to George McClain, who finds me down the court. As I attempted to go up for a layup with 9 seconds left on the clock, I got fouled, and now I had to go to the line. Now, the crazy part of the story was that at the time, Cozell McQueen, who had been playing all game, hadn't scored a single point and was lined up to the left of the basket. I take my shot, I miss, but the ball bounces right to him for the rebound; he shoots and ties the game. Pepperdine still had 5 seconds left on the clock but could not score, and we ended up going into double overtime and winning the game by 2 points, 69-67.

Pepperdine was a tough opponent, but we managed to survive and moved on to play in the second round against another legendary coach, Jerry Tarkanian, and the UNLV Runnin' Rebels. Before the game, UNLV star player Sidney Green had been trash-talking about my teammate Thurl Bailey in the newspapers, saying things like, "Yeah, I watched the game last night, and he didn't impress me" and "I ain't worried about Bailey." But Bailey never let any of it get to his head. Green was trying to punk Thurl Bailey because he thought he was soft. And for a while, UNLV was getting the best of us. They managed to get as high as a 12-point lead on us, but like in our previous games, we had them right where we wanted them. We continued playing hard, and with just 2 seconds left, Thurl Bailey outrebounded Sidney Green, scoring the winning basket and leading us to a 71-70. We survived, advanced, and then played in Ogden, Utah, at Weaver State against the University of Utah in the Regional Semifinal, where we got an easy win, 75-56. Once again, I ran over to Coach Valvano and gave him his hug. Whether it was an easy win or not, it was one step closer to the Final Four. The more we won, the more support multiplied. I vividly remember how much the fans enjoyed the journey we were taking them on. They came from all over the country to watch us play. Even the owner, Mr. George Hall of Virginia Crabtree Women's Clothing store, where I worked, drove from North Carolina to Utah to watch us play. We were on fire! And everyone just wanted to be there to see us.

Here's a quick story! While working at Virginia Crabtree during my junior year, the owner, George Hall, had a 1974 NC State Championship team plaque behind his desk. I remember going over to Mr. Hall and saying, "You know something? I'm tired of looking at that plaque." I'm going to get my own plaque one day." And now we were battling it out in the tournament, trying to win it all. They started calling us "The Team of Destiny." But who's there waiting for us? Ralph Sampson and the Virginia

Cavaliers, again. All the reporters from the East thought this would be the moment that Three Time Player of the Year Ralph Sampson finally got to the Final Four. We knew they were going to come even harder this time after we had beat them in the ACC Championship game. Virginia didn't consider us a threat and felt we got lucky when we beat them two weeks prior; they might have even been looking forward to who they would be playing against next in the semifinal game after beating us. But regardless of what they were thinking, we came to play hard and win.

We knew nothing easy about going up against Ralph Sampson again, but we wouldn't let him run all over us either. Remember this: Sidney Lowe and I came from a high school where we were used to winning. When you get to the point where you expect to win, you will be unshaken by the moment. People who haven't experienced that will never understand that feeling. We did. And it wasn't just Sidney and me. We had a team of warriors who felt the same way. From the outside, everyone could only see the surface of the great Ralph Sampson, but we competed. Anytime you compete, anything can happen. If there is one thing sports will teach you, anyone can come back at any moment, and the game is over once the clock runs out.

Virginia's most significant lead was 7 points in the second half, but we still had 7 minutes to play, which we felt was more than enough time to come back and win. We managed to stick around, and by the time the game clock got down to about 1 minute and 28 seconds, I made a jump shot over Othell Wilson, tying the score. Again, with the shot clock rule, Virginia chose to hold the ball, and we're playing for the last shot. With 55 seconds left on the clock, Coach Valvano tells us to foul them. Who calls for that when the game is tied? Well, it's worked for us before, so why not? I went and fouled Othell Wilson, who was a 72% free throw shooter. He makes the first free throw, misses the second, and Thurl Bailey grabs the rebound. Once we got the ball across the court, I got a pass and drove into the paint, and when I saw Ralph Sampson coming in, I dished a pass to Lorenzo

Charles, who ended up getting fouled and going to the line to shoot free throws. Although Lorenzo Charles could have been a better free throw shooter, Coach Valvano spoke to us as if he knew he would make both shots. Charles goes and sinks the first one, ties the score 62-62, and now has the chance to make one more to put us in the lead.

He sinks it in, and we go up by one. But Virginia still has 23 seconds on the clock. We knew they would try to get the ball to Ralph Sampson, but by the time they got across the court, we had almost the entire team around him, making it practically impossible to get the ball to him. "Don't let Ralph get the ball" is all I heard. With 7 seconds on the clock, Virginia's Tim Mullen shoots the ball, bouncing off the rim and into his teammate Othell Wilson's hands. Out of desperation, Wilson takes a shot, but it comes up short, and the clock runs out. We win the game by one point, 63-62. No one knew that Virginia's bench had been heckling me whenever I had the ball. So, after we won, I got caught up in the moment, ran over and celebrated right in front of Virginia's bench, and yelled, "Go home." It's years later, and I still regret doing that. I got caught up in the moment.

We beat The Great Ralph Sampson and the Number 1 team in the country twice after losing to them seven times in a row. It was just pandemonium; it was unbelievable! I was named the MVP of the Western Regionals. After the game, about 90% of the reporters who came to Albuquerque expecting Ralph Sampson to win left. The reason why we realized that was because 30 years later, while we were filming the Survive and Advance documentary, we did some research on all the reporters that we thought were in Albuquerque to get their take on the game and were able only to find just a few because most of them had left right after the game. They weren't there for us; they were there for Sampson. Ultimately, it doesn't matter who believes in you if you believe in yourself. Believers will come along eventually, which took only a short time.

We had been on the road for ten days and could finally fly back home to North Carolina. When we got back to the airport in North Carolina, there were 2000 people out there waiting to congratulate us. The fans were going wild, cheering us on. Then, when we got on the bus to head to our campus, hundreds more were hanging out over the bridge and on the side of the highway. It was an incredible feeling to see them all out there. It got even crazier once we returned to the gym for practice. I couldn't believe what I was seeing. When we went to practice at Reynolds Coliseum, there were 5 thousand fans in attendance to watch us practice. I asked Coach Valvano, "What are all these people doing here?" Coach V turned and put his arms around me and said, "Just enjoy it."

We even had a pep rally where another 6 to 7 thousand people came to celebrate with us. I couldn't believe it because Coach Valvano was usually very serious when it came to practice. He always wanted us to focus. That day, he wanted the security at our campus to let them all in so they could be a part of it. Once, he told us to "Just enjoy it; he managed it so well." We went along with it. That was just the kind of person our coach was. He always wanted to make practice fun, and he always made sure we were focused and that we understood our roles. No one will ever understand just how powerful that was for our fans. There is no coach that I could think of that would have ever done that. We thought it was wild as the crowd cheered as we made our layups during practice. We were all living in the moment and happy to be in the position that we were in. We were closer to winning the National Championship, just as Coach Valvano dreamed.

Pep Rally at NC State

We respected each other in everything that we did as a team. Sidney was our quarterback and leader; Thurl was our spirit, and I was the lion. If anyone messed with us, I was the one to let them have it. I was the enforcer, and everybody knew that. The great thing about our team was that we all understood each other. No one was there to outshine anybody else. If you looked at all the other teams, they all had one thing in common. They had individual stars. We didn't have that. We were all equal, making it hard for teams to beat us. When it came to the teams we played against, we knew who to try to shut down; they didn't know how to respond once you took away their biggest weapons. That's how we beat Sampson twice, not to mention that we had one of the best strategic coaches on our side.

We were now in the Final Four, and Georgia was our next opponent. Before heading back out West, I remember Coach Valvano telling us to "Pack as if you're not coming home." That was such a tremendous psychological thing to put in our thoughts. He had a remarkable ability to motivate us through situations where he made everything seem possible. Coach Valvano always made us feel as if we could accomplish the impossible. We believed in him so much that we never wanted to disappoint him. It was as if he lived through a script and knew all the outcomes beforehand. His dream of winning the National Championship seemed prophesied because he had led us to the Final Four. Remember, we had already practiced cutting down the nets.

It was Coach's third year, and we knew that if we didn't win the NCAA Championship, the pressure he would have to face would weigh heavily on him. We wanted to make sure that we not only made it to the championship game but also to win it all and cut the net down like he had envisioned. Many people didn't understand the position he was in. He was an oddball. Remember, he was an Italian from New York coaching in the South in the early 80s. It wasn't like he was the cool guy on the block. But people grew to like him. As much as many people doubted him as a coach when he first arrived, now, everyone was coming from all over the country to see us play because when you win, everyone likes you. Next, we were back out west in Albuquerque, New Mexico, getting ready to play the Georgia Bulldogs.

Chapter 13

The Dream

Georgia, who had a great team, had just upset the North Carolina Tar Heels. It sometimes crosses my mind and makes me wonder what the outcome would have been if we had played against North Carolina in the semifinal game instead of playing against Georgia. I'm sure it would have been a tough matchup, and fans all over North Carolina would have enjoyed that, but it was now our turn to play Georgia and try to win so we could play in the championship game. The year prior, in 1982, Georgia's star player, Dominique Wilkins, had left to go and play in the NBA in his junior season. Playing against him would have been tough, too. However, they still had good players like Vern Fleming and James Banks, their leading scorers. We knew we had to focus on them first to advance.

Most people across the country weren't paying attention to our game against Georgia. They were all tuning in to watch the Houston Cougars against the Louisville Cardinals because both teams were very athletic, and they also knew it would be a dunk fest. Earlier in the season, we had lost to Louisville by 5 points in Louisville, but we had never played against Houston. Either way, we didn't care who we ended up playing against. All we knew was that we just wanted to get to the championship and win it all. According to all the experts, our game against Georgia was considered the Cinderella versus Cinderella matchup, and the winner would go and play against King Kong. In the end, although Georgia had outscored us in the second half, they came up short, and we managed to beat them by 7 points. What was so ironic about playing Georgia was that back in 1979, Sidney and I were playing on the Washington DC AAU team, and we had lost to Georgia's AAU team, which had some of the same players we were playing against in the Final Four one of them being their center, the late Terry Fair.

We were now just one step closer, and we could feel it. I ran over to Coach Valvano and gave him another big hug. After our win against Georgia, we all returned to our hotel and watched the Houston versus Louisville game. As predicted, that game was a dunk fest. They were dunking on each other and blocking each other's shots throughout the game. It was a very entertaining game. I'm pretty sure that everyone across the country watched that game. It was a game based on athleticism. There was no other game that could compare to the excitement that it brought to the fans. It was probably one of the highest-rated games because of so much athleticism. But like I said, we didn't care who we had to play. We were just happy to be there. Houston ended up beating Louisville 94-81, and now, it was our turn to play them in the championship game.

We practiced the very next day. Out of nowhere, I had come down with flu-like symptoms. I practiced, but I was not feeling well at all. They had decided to take my roommate Alvin Battle out of the room for the day to keep him from getting sick. Minutes before that, Harry Bynum, a representative for PONY shoes, dropped off a pair of sneakers in hopes that I would wear them for our game. They were a good-looking pair of shoes.

I will never forget that while I was laying down sick in my room, I got a knock on the door. It's my dad. He comes in and asks, "How are you feeling, son?" I told him I was coming down with a cold but was "ok." He then asked, "Are you going to be ready for the championship game?" I said, "Absolutely," and he just walked out the door. That was it. It was like he was saying, "You better be ready." My dad just had that sense of quietness, but I felt he came there to encourage me to work through it so I could play. But in my mind, there was no doubt I would play. It was not only the championship game; it was my last college game, and there was no way I would sit it out.

The dream of getting to the championship was now a reality. Although I had worn my Shell Toe Adidas all year, I decided to go out there wearing my brand-new PONY shoes. I was mentally prepared to win and cut down the nets as we had rehearsed during practice all year. Before our game, as we were going over the game plan, Coach Valvano looked around and said to us, "The hell with this game plan; we know what to do; let's just go out there and kick their butts; we're not going to hold the ball, we're going to go out there and go right after them." That was our game plan. Right before we huddled up and went out there on the court, one of the former players from the 1974 NC State Championship Team, Phil Spence, came bursting through our locker room door and said, "Let's go, let's go, we can win this thing, let's go." Talk about giving us the boost we needed. Suddenly, I was no longer feeling sick. My adrenalin was high, and I felt like I was in a movie.

After talking about it all year, we were facing the Houston Cougars, and all I could think was, "Coach Valvano was right all along." Now, it was game time. And let me say no one ever expected us to be there. Think about this for a minute. Back then, no one in the college basketball world thought we could beat Virginia and the great Ralph Sampson. Now imagine how everyone felt after they realized that we would be playing against Houston. They had two future NBA Hall of Famers, Hakeem Olajuwon, and Clyde Drexler, on their team, who also would be later named on the list of the top 75 players in the game's history. But like the story of David and Goliath, our faith was strong, and Coach Valvano was on our side.

Houston was nicknamed Phi Slama Jama due to their acrobatic ways of dunking. After watching them beat Louisville, we knew that Olajuwon would be a big problem for us. Houston was known as a team that made a lot of dunks. Part of our game plan was to keep Houston from transitioning to where they could dunk the ball because once they started dunking, it was over. It motivated them, and we knew that if we could stop them from doing it, we could mentally take them out of their game. Before the game, Coach Valvano told us that the team with the most dunks would win. It did not make sense to us before the game, but that became our mission.

The funny thing was that Coach Valvano had been teasing the media all week and telling them, "We were going to hold the ball all game and might not take a shot until Tuesday." It was his way of trying to fool Houston because that was never the case; the game plan was the opposite. Once on the court, we ran all over the place, shooting the ball. Even though most of our shots weren't going in, Houston may have been startled by our aggression. We were taking more shots than they were. We went at them right from the tip-off. They weren't expecting that from us. We were in total control of the tempo.

We were up by eight at halftime, 33-25. One of the main reasons we had the lead was that Clyde Drexler had four fouls and had to sit out for a very long time. This would never have happened had we held the ball passively. We were pumped but not overly excited in the locker room because we knew the game wasn't over. Coach Valvano seemed calm and poised, knowing we still had another half to play. He just reminded us that they would come out and try to make a run but not to worry because we were going to make a run, too. So, we came out in the second half, Clyde Drexler was still sitting on the bench, and they decided they would get the ball down to Olajuwon. And that's where the problems started. We had no answer for him. We tried to do everything possible to slow him down, but nothing worked. They not only caught up to us, but they also went on to take the lead. They came out with a 17-2 run, but Coach Valvano never panicked. He reminded us of what we always talked about and said, "Be in a position to win at the end of the game." Suddenly, another critical thing happened. Olajuwon got so tired he needed to go out and get some oxygen. In the meantime, Houston was trying to hold the ball to give Olajuwon time to recover and catch his breath. And that's when we started to come back and catch up. But Houston never gave up. They managed to come back and retake the lead. That's when we went to what had been working all along for us, we started fouling.

We were down two, and we fouled freshman Alvin Franklin; he then went to the line and missed the one-and-one. We got the rebound and went in transition; Sidney Lowe found me in the corner with 1 minute and 54 seconds left. I put up a jumper, and we tied the score 52-52. Once Houston inbounded the ball, we waited for Franklin to get the ball again so we could foul because we felt he was the perfect target. And again, he missed his free throw. We managed to get the rebound and called a timeout. During the timeout, we discussed holding the ball until we could take the last shot. We had designed this play called "The Five Play," where Sidney would have the ball on top, Thurl Bailey and I were to his right, and we got the double screen with Cozell McQueen and Lorenzo Charles on the left side. We would run Thurl Bailey off a double screen going to the left, and Sidney Lowe would look at him, and on the other side, I would have a one-on-one opportunity, or a lob play because I would be on that side all by myself. That was the play that we had designed. When we came out of the huddle and onto the court, we noticed they were in a one-three-one-trap. We didn't anticipate that. Any other coach would have panicked and called another timeout, but Coach just let it play out. That was the genius of Coach Valvano. A key trait of being a great coach is knowing when and when not to coach. He just let us play those final seconds out. Regardless of what Houston was doing, we decided to pass the ball around until one of us could get open to take a shot. Honestly, after the "five play" failed, we didn't have a play.

Houston had plenty of opportunities to force us to turn over the ball, but remember, basketball is not a thinking game; it's a reaction game. Everything happens in seconds. You don't have time to sit around and think, you must react. No matter how well you design a play, you never know what the defense will do. So, we only considered the game clock the entire time we passed the ball around. Once we saw that we had gotten it down to the last 10 seconds, Sidney passed the ball down to Thurl Bailey in the corner, but not only did he see Hakeem Olajuwon coming towards him, he hadn't made a shot in the second quarter. He quickly realized he had no option other than to make a one-handed cross-court pass to me almost 35 feet away from the basket, which Benny Anders almost stole. Thank God my DeMatha High School coach, Morgan Wootten, taught me the fundamentals of catching the ball with two hands because had that not been the case, Anders would have stolen the ball and ended the game with a dunk.

Once I could get two hands on the ball, I knew I had to get it up there. I had to take my shot because the clock had only four seconds left. Judging from where I was, as the ball arced towards the basket, it looked like it was heading directly towards its target and had a great shot at going in. Hakeem Olajuwon was jostling for position under the basket, and Lorenzo Charles was behind him. For some reason, Olajuwon stood there watching the ball heading towards the basket. With just two seconds left, Lorenzo Charles jumps up, grabs "the pass" in midair, and dunks it in, and we win as time expires. Houston just stood around the basket, looking stunned. That game ranked 26th in the most memorable moments in sports history. And guess what? Ultimately, we had two dunks, and Houston only had one. As Coach Valvano said, whoever has the most dunks at the end of the game will win. To this day, I wonder how the hell he knew that. That dunk is probably the most memorable dunk of all time. After realizing we had just won the game, we were all just celebrating as Coach Valvano ran around the court, looking for me to give him his post-victory hug, but I was nowhere to be found. He later said, "I was running around looking for Dereck Whittenburg and for the first time in 10 games, he's hugging someone else".

1983 National Champions

I ran over to hug my parents but only saw my mom. I don't know where my father was. After hugging her, I ran back to the court, and when Coach Valvano saw me, he asked, "Where were you? "I was looking all over for you to give you a hug." I gave him a big hug, and then we went and cut down the nets just like he had always planned. I loved Coach Valvano so much that I even kissed him on his cheek during the press conference.

I mentioned that play to Olajuwon while filming the Survive and Advance documentary, and he explained to me that he thought had he gone to grab the ball while in midair, the officials would have called him for a goaltending violation. Looking back, Olajuwon, four inches taller than Charles, could have easily stripped Charles of the ball. He didn't want to risk it. Had he got to it before Charles, we would have gone into overtime, and Lord knows what the outcome would have been. Luckily for us, he didn't, and we were able to score the winning basket; the rest is history. By not calling a timeout, Coach Valvano forced the game action to dictate the result. His decision forced Olajuwon to play according to his plan. We also held Clyde Drexler to just 4 points because he was in foul trouble throughout the game. That was likely due to their reaction to our stealth strategy, which was to come out aggressive. Both strategies showed Coach Valvano's coaching brilliance. I tease Drexler every chance I get and say to him, "Hey, you let us win that championship. That's why you and Olajuwon won two NBA world championships together as Houston Rockets. Losing to us made you hungry."

The one thing that most people did not notice was that although Sidney and I seemed very excited that we had won, Thurl Bailey looked like he was in shock. He had this look on his face. "We did it." Sidney, Coach Valvano, and I knew it was possible. At least us three, for sure. No offense to anybody on our team, but we knew it was possible. We were happy that we had won, but not surprised. Between Coach Valvano's dream and Sidney and my history of winning, we never doubted we could win. We came there to win the national championship. We didn't go there with the dream to make it to the NBA. Belief is powerful.

After the game, Commentators Billy Packer and Brent Musburger interviewed the three seniors, me, Sidney Lowe, and Thurl Bailey. I remember Musbuger asking me, "What happened at the end of the play?" I joked and said, "It was a great pass; that play was designed for Lorenzo Charles. I told him to be ready for it," and everyone laughed. To this day, everywhere I go, people always ask me, "Was it a shot or pass?" Some people say it was destiny, some said it was a miracle, we say we had the chemistry and thought we could win it all. Our coach had said to us from day one that we would win the National Championship, and we did. That last play became such a good joke that I have "It was a pass" stitched on my golf bag. I was named MVP for the CBS game for NC State, while Hakeem Olajuwon was the MVP for Houston, as well as the MVP of the NCAA Tournament. It was a crazy journey that started in the ACC Tournament against Wake Forest and ended with us winning it all in the 1983 National Championship against Houston. In total, we won 10 consecutive games, which started with our final home game against Wake Forest. At the time, we were the lowest seed ever to win the national championship and the first team to win the title away from our region. We ended the season with a record 26-10 and 16th in the AP poll. Our run is considered the most famous in college basketball history.

Celebrating with Teammates and Coach V

Here are some little-known facts that people may not know about our 1983 National Championship Team. We were the first National Championship Team for Nike. The reason why I know that is because when I used to visit the John McEnroe building, which was in the same building as then Nike CEO Phil Knight's office, there was a plaque on the wall that said, 1983 NC State Championship Team, Jim Valvano Coach, The First Championship Team for Nike. Even though they might have been a little upset with us for wearing Adidas and PONYS during the National Championship game, the plaque still adorned the wall. Most will also remember when Sports Illustrated referenced our 1983 Championship Team as delivering the greatest college basketball moment of the 20th Century. Of course, Lorenzo Charles' famous dunk and Coach Valvano running around the court after our win remain unforgettable.

"My dream was always to cut the nets down in the National Championship.
Coach Jimmy Valvano

Chapter 14

The White House

When we returned to North Carolina from Albuquerque, everyone was just going crazy. Everyone made us feel like we were the Beatles or Michael Jackson when we came through. We couldn't go anywhere without the fans wanting to celebrate with us. We were on top of the world and could do no wrong. We were like rock stars. There wasn't a single place where we would go where people wouldn't recognize us. The celebration continued through the remainder of our semester and through the summer. We went barnstorming and touring North Carolina, meeting all the fans and having the time of our lives. All the seniors from the ACC would assemble a team, and we would play each other in exhibition games where the fans would pay to watch us play. The fans loved it because they saw us play up close compared to watching us on television. People would recognize us; they wanted to take pictures and ask us for our autographs. It felt like we partied for an entire year. It was just such a special time for all of us. Being a part of the team and that historical run was a great experience.

One of my most memorable moments was going down to Channel 5 in North Carolina as a team and talking live to then-President Ronald Reagan. Things weren't the same back then as today, where a championship team physically goes to the White House and meets the president in person.

After Coach Valvano spoke to the President, the camera turned to our team, and I was allowed to speak. Coach Valvano had this look on his face like, *"What in the hell is Whitt going to say?"* He looked worried because he didn't know what I would ask the President. He just knew I was probably going to say something crazy. I looked into the camera and asked the President, "Can I get a summer job flying F-15 fighter jets?" Everyone laughed about it. I was always fascinated with flying fighter jets, and I thought it was cool to say to the President.

Shortly after that, Coach Valvano, Sidney Lowe, and I were personally invited to go down to the White House along with our high school coach Morgan Wootten, Bob Geoghan, who ran the McDonald's All-American Games, and Jan Russ, who was a part of the Department of Interior to meet President Ronald Reagan in person. I thought it was very ironic that I was standing inside the White House because it brought me back to when I used to tell my music teacher, Mrs. Harris, that I wanted to become President. Of course, I didn't become President, but I thought it was cool that I was standing beside President Reagan. We were there to celebrate the National Championship at NC State, but what made it even more special was that Sidney and I were two kids from the DC area who had also won the National Championship at DeMatha High School. Think about it. In the history of sports, name two guys who were teammates who won a National Championship in high school and played together and won a National Championship in college. *I bet you might never find one.* It was just a good look for DC and the White House. Not to mention that although Thurl Bailey wasn't there with us at the White House during the visit, he, too, was also from the DC area and played a major part on our team. Looking back, I believe we took that visit for granted, and because of the natural high we were on, we couldn't take it all in. That was such a big moment.

Meeting President Ronald Reagan

How many of you knew we were the first team in the ACC (Atlantic Coast Conference) to win the national championship game with five black starters? Also, it was the first final four, where all four teams had five black starters. Now, what if I told you that the date we won the championship was April 4, 1983, exactly 15 years from the date of Martin Luther King Jr's assassination? Pretty interesting, isn't it? We weren't far removed from that kind of change. I believe that's very powerful.

After driving by the White House for so many years, I was now looking at it inside the Oval Office. It was such an awesome experience. All I could think was, *"I never thought I would ever be in the White House."* Imagine. How many people in their lifetime get an opportunity to go to the White House and meet the President? Back then, that was unheard of. It wasn't like I just got up one day and said, "You know what, one day, *I'm just going to go to the White House and meet the President."* Some people may take that lightly, but it was a big deal to me.

President Reagan was such a character. He was teasing and making us laugh the entire time. We took a picture together and chatted for a little bit about the National Championship and spoke about how proud he was of how we represented DC. The visit lasted about 30 minutes, but that memory will last a lifetime for me. Thirty years later, in 2013, I came up with the idea that our 1983 National Championship team should visit the White House. We did not visit in 1983 after winning the championship because it would have been an NCAA violation. I failed to reach the right people until Thurl Bailey, who was living in Utah, informed me that he knew the late Senator Orin Hatch, who had a good relationship with President Barack Obama, and that's how we finally got it invited. President Obama, too, was a character just like President Ronald Reagan. I thought it was funny when he stood before us and said, "Sorry, I'm not wearing red," then we handed him an NC State jersey with the number 1 on it. President Obama said, *All of us remember that game as one of the greatest games of all time, and that image of Coach Valvano running through the court is still one that is seared in everyone's memory."* That was a huge moment for us as a team. It was just such a great experience for all of us.

Meeting President Barack Obama

Chapter 15

Just Business

My entire experience at NC State University, both as a student and as an athlete, was wonderful. I mostly remember all the faculty and staff that impacted me while I was there. For example, Dr. Joe Brown, who was one of the academic advisors in the athletic department, would always encourage me to meet with the professors after class if there was anything I didn't understand. I credit Dr. Jack Wilson, my academic advisor on campus, as someone I spent a lot of time with and encouraged me in my studies. Dr. Wandra Hill, who was in the mathematics department, would say encouraging words whenever she saw me. My sports History professors and two of my favorite people, Dr. Joe Hobbs and Dr. Beasley, greatly impacted me. Finally, we have the Registrar, Joan Bird. She was the most important person to me when I was in school because she was the one who collected all the information, knew all your grades and your GPA, and was the final person who would say to you that you are officially graduating. No students at any school will know or can tell you who their registrar is, but I will never forget mine.

During my last year, I was really concerned about graduating. It was now April, and I still had the remainder of what was left of my senior year, as well as preparing myself for what was next. Graduating for me was such a big deal, not only for me personally, but also for my family. We're talking about the late 1970's. Going to a major college was considered a great accomplishment back then. Getting a college scholarship at that level and graduating as a first-generation graduate was huge back then. In the meantime, I looked forward to graduating to the next big thing, the NBA.

At the time, I was represented by Agent David Faulk from Proserv Agency out of Washington, DC. I was told that there was a possibility that I could be a high pick in the draft. I was a part of the 1979 high school class, one of the greatest classes in basketball history. You had Ralph Sampson, Isaiah Thomas, James Worthy, Dominique Wilkins, Clyde Drexler, Sam Bouie, and Sidney Green, of which four of these seven players were later named to the list of the top 75 greatest NBA players of all time. The draft wasn't as big an event as it is today. You pretty much had to do everything on your own. Today, your agent gets you all the workouts, gets you a trainer, and stays in contact with most of the NBA teams. We did not have any of that provided to us back then.

I made sure I worked out to stay in shape all the way up until the draft. I was very excited to be in New York, sitting in the green room with the rest of the players waiting to be drafted. We had just won the National Championship; I was the MVP and a very popular guy with many people cheering for me. There was no one with me in New York except for my agent. The first and second rounds came and went, and my name hadn't been called. I'm sitting there thinking, "Shit, when am I going to get drafted?" I thought I was a good player and should have been picked. The third round comes around, and I finally get picked by the Phoenix Suns. Everyone was cheering for me, but I must admit, I was disappointed. I wasn't angry, just disappointed. I wasn't disappointed in being drafted by the Suns, but because of how long it took. That's when reality hit me.

So, I get drafted by the Suns and sign my contract. To be honest, I had no idea what I was signing. I knew it was a contract for the Phoenix Suns, but that's all I knew. We then went to pre-training camp, where we had players like Kyle Macy, Walter Davis, and Maurice Lucas, who were all established starters on the team. At the time, we were just running around and playing pick-up games, and I was killing these guys. I will never forget Walter Davis saying, "That's the golden guy. You keep beating up on Kyle Macy, and I don't know if they will let you make this team." But I was going hard at everybody there at the camp.

Training camp lasted about a week and a half, and I was out there trying to prove that I was good enough to be on the team. I went through the entire process, and I was doing pretty good. Long story short, I get cut. Now, let me explain to you just how cruel the world is. After our workout, we hopped on the bus to return to the hotel. The bus driver pulls into the hotel parking lot, parks the bus, and Assistant Coach Al Bianchi walks over to me and says, "Yeah, man, you got cut; *you're not going to make the team.*" There was no type of love involved in that moment. There's no professionalism in professional sports. Although I felt confident, they had me trying to be a point guard instead of trying out for my natural shooting guard position. I truly feel that had they tried me out as a shooting guard, I would have made the team. However, maybe that was just a way to make it easier for them to cut me. I was more like a Joe Dumars type of player back then, but there weren't too many players my size playing the shooting guard position. If I came out today with the talent I had back then, there is no doubt that I would be a superstar in the NBA. I attribute my not being prepared or trained to play point guard as a big reason for my being cut. I did not have the mindset to play the point guard position. Ultimately, I make no excuses because I should have been prepared to go out and do whatever it took to make the team.

I returned home to North Carolina, floating around, trying to keep myself in shape. In the meantime, I returned to school because I still had a few classes to complete to graduate and get my degree. I started working in Fuquay-Varina, North Carolina, at a textile plant, which was a neat experience. I got the job through an alumnus and would drive there thrice a week after practice. My responsibilities there were to monitor people's productivity and keep an eye on the machines. Although I wanted to get back on the basketball court, I still had to continue focusing on the present, my education, and my job until an opportunity to play presented.

Although I didn't make it in the NBA, it didn't mean I would give up and lay in my bed staring at the ceiling for the rest of my life. I wanted to keep playing, but I also had to remember that my life wasn't over simply because the Suns had cut me. Many athletes put so much hope and effort, both emotionally and physically, into making it into professional sports that they feel they are failures if they don't get drafted. That is not the right outlook. You can't feel your life is over or that you are doomed because you didn't reach the next level. Growing up, we were always told to never put all our eggs in one basket. Today, when it comes to sports, that seems to be what most athletes are doing. There is just so much pressure on athletes these days to make it that if they do not, they become depressed and feel that life is over. Being an athlete is only a small part of who you are; it doesn't define you. You can be considered a great athlete, but you can do much more, even if things don't go as planned.

Going to college helps to prepare you, but hopefully, you're also leaving with an education. The premise of using basketball and not letting it use you is the mindset every athlete should have in case their dreams of making it to the NBA don't happen. If you put your mind to it, you have an entire life to succeed at whatever you choose. As much as I did not like being cut by the Phoenix Suns, I had to understand that it was just business. I never felt deterred by it or felt that my life was over. I wasn't thinking about forcing the issue or continuing to try out. I immediately started preparing myself for the next step. Did I want to be in the NBA? Of course, I did. But I'm one of the few guys in basketball history who can say they won a National Championship in high school and college. Although I did not make it to the NBA, I am the perfect example of someone who can say to the 99% of athletes who don't make it that although your dreams of making it may not happen, there is so much more to success in life. You must focus on what you want to become and pursue it with the same passion you gave to being an athlete. Sports are great, but you must keep it in perspective. I never doubted that I was good enough to play in the NBA, but forcing myself to continuously try out was not something I was willing to do.

Chapter 16

Playing Overseas

While taking my last classes at NC State, Coach Valvano received a phone call telling him there was a tryout camp at St. Peters College in New Jersey for the Le Mans basketball team, an overseas team in France. Although dedicated to graduating, I still wanted to pursue my basketball career. Coach Valvano told me I should go and take a shot at it because it was a good opportunity for me if I wanted to continue playing. I was still in pretty good shape, so I went along. I flew up to New Jersey and when I arrived, I went and met with the Le Mans coach, Kenny Grant. Once I got on the court, I noticed about 160 players were trying out, and about 140 were guards. Out of the 160 players, they were only looking to choose just 5 players. I tried out, and I did well. I was invited to go to France. The funny thing was that after thinking I had already made the team, Coach Grant turned to me while on our flight to France and told me that I hadn't made the team yet.

When I arrived, they had other American players on the team that I had to try and beat out. There would be a series of exhibition games where you had to compete against other Americans. It was set up so that one player would play the first half, and the next would play in the second half. Imagine how much pressure that is knowing that the player that went before you performed well and scored many points. Now, you must play harder and outscore them. And not to mention, we also had to try to win the game. That's a whole lot of pressure! In the end, the team had 2 Americans per team. The player I had to compete against was Jim Johnstone from Wake Forest.

After competing for my position, I was able to make the team. The good thing about playing overseas is that the money you made was tax-free, you didn't have to pay for the apartment, you had a food voucher, and they also gave you a car to get around. While playing in Europe, I also discovered many great players you would never imagine were over there. I was playing against some guys I had never heard of that were unbelievable players. Everyone always seems to think that the best players are all playing in the NBA, but there are so many great players all over Europe. It was an eye-opening experience for me.

Le Mans France (1984)

I was now living in another country for the first time in my life and had to learn the language. For me to communicate better, I went and hired a tutor to help me. Being away from home while at NC State was one thing, but being in another country was another experience. It got lonely over there. I didn't have much to do throughout the day except play basketball. I remember my mom giving me a Bible that I began reading every night before bed. My biggest expense became my phone bill from always calling home. The smartest thing I did was set up a bank account back in the States, so every time I would get paid, I would send most of it back because I feared spending it. I would only keep enough to live off in the meantime.

The most shocking thing I had to deal with while playing for Le Mans occurred during a European Tournament in the 1984-1985 season. Before one of our games in Belgium, I was approached by a player on the opposing team facing elimination. He approached me and asked if I would throw *the game for 5 thousand dollars, and I immediately told him, "Nah man, I'm not doing that," and* then walked away from him. I became so upset that I immediately went to my coach to let him know about it. I had never in my life been asked to throw a game. The crazy thing was that I never accepted the money and still played poorly, and it probably did look like I was throwing the game.

The team and the city really liked me. I went around to the schools and did many things in the community to try and fit in. They even made little dolls of me for the fans. It was interesting while I was out there. We ended up having an ok season but didn't make it to any tournaments or win the championship. I was the team's leading scorer and felt I had it good after the season. The owners were trying to have me sign a lucrative contract while also trying to recruit bigger French players to build the team around me. But for some reason, I didn't want to continue playing basketball in Europe anymore. Being away in another country wasn't easy; I just wanted to return home and finish my degree. I always stayed in touch with Coach Valvano during my time in Europe. I explained to him that I was contemplating my career and whether I wanted to continue playing basketball and discussed the possibility of me becoming a coach somewhere. I had to really think about what I wanted to do with my future. After playing just one year in France, I was at a crossroads. I didn't know if I wanted to play overseas or begin my coaching career. Although playing in France was a great experience that allowed me to travel, I was no longer interested in chasing after basketball. One day, Coach Valvano called and asked me, *"Do you want to come back and begin your coaching career?"*

After considering it, I said, *"Why not start coaching now instead of flying back and forth to Europe for the next 5 or 6 years"*. And just like that, my career as a player ended, and my new journey as a coach began. I returned to NC State to coach as a graduate assistant and finish my degree. I was Coach Valvano's assistant coach for one year for the 1985-1986 season. While I was coaching, I would go around and work at basketball camps where I would do some shooting exhibitions and give speeches about basketball and how to get better as a player. Although I loved to play the game of basketball, I always had an interest in coaching, dating back to when I worked at summer camps with Coach Wootten, so I felt that coaching would be a great career for me. It was embedded in me, and I had great experiences from watching great coaches. My influence on coaching came from my mentors, who showed me how to become a great coach.

Assistant Coach to Coach V (Right of picture)

During my freshman and sophomore years at NC State, I worked at a few basketball camps and did some speaking engagements at George Mason University in Fairfax, Virginia. Those camps were operated by Coach Red Jenkins, the head coach at WT Woodson High School, where Duke University standout Tommy Amaker played, and Coach Joe Harrington, the head coach at George Mason University who played for the legendary Coach Lefty Driesell at the University of Maryland and was his assistant coach for ten years. After my speech at the camp, Coach Joe Harrington approached me and said, *"Man, I would love for you to come back and work with me if you ever want to get into coaching."* I told him, "I would love to," and I had always kept that in my mind. One year after being a graduate assistant coach at NC State, I started looking for an opportunity to coach full-time. Not that I wasn't happy at NC State. I was engaged to be married then, and on April 19, 1986, my wife of 38 years, Jacqueline Williams, and I married in her hometown of Raleigh. Coach Harrington attended our wedding. He and I spoke briefly about maybe one day working together. Not too long after that, he called to let me know he had an opening for a full-time assistant coach position and told me he would love for me to come and work with him. I accepted the position and became his assistant at George Mason. It was my first full-time assistant coaching job.

Shortly after accepting the position, my wife and I moved to Vienna, Virginia, a suburb of Washington, DC, close to George Mason University. There weren't many people who looked like us living in Vienna. In fact, although I had lived in the DC area and Glenarden, Maryland, we never had any reason to ever go across to Virginia. Back in those days, no Blacks were living in that area. But now, I was living there. Every day, I would have to drive across Route 123 to get to George Mason in Fairfax, Virginia. It was about a 15-minute ride from my house. I loved it because it was nearby, and I could still go and recruit in the DC area. The only problem was that I would get pulled over seemingly about twice a week. *"Sir, what are you doing around this area?"* the officers would always ask me. After explaining to them that I lived in Vienna as I handed them my driver's license, they would always go back, run my name, and then come back and ask me, *"Are you the Dereck Whittenburg that went to DeMatha High School and NC State?"* When I would say yes, they would turn to me and say, *"OK, man, see you later, have a great night,"* and walk away. That must have happened to me at least 20 times from different cops. I was just being pulled over for no reason. Of course, they never came out and said it, but I knew for sure I was being profiled for being Black.

After coaching at George Mason for one year, Coach Harrington was hired as the head coach at Long Beach State, so I went with him to California to be his assistant coach. While I was on the West Coast, I heard they were forming a group called the Black Coaches Association and I had been asked to attend their first meeting. Honestly, I had no idea what the association was about. I was just very curious, and I wanted to go and be a part of it. Occasionally, I would go and visit George Raveling, who at the time was the head coach at USC and was one of the only Black coaches I knew in the area. He was an avid reader, a great motivational speaker, and a very intelligent man. He's the one who taught me the importance of reading books. He was also a founding member of the Black Coaches Association. Joe Harrington, who is White and really respected me as a person, was the one who encouraged me to join the organization because he felt it was very important for me to become involved.

Assistant Coach to Coach Harrington

The Black Coaches Association was formed by Georgetown Head Coach John Thompson, Harry Edwards, an activist in the 1960s and a professor at the University of California at Berkeley, and Rudy Washington, also from California. The association was formed because, in 1987, there were few black head coaches in traditionally white schools nationwide. It was really an injustice what they were doing to Black coaches during that time because they weren't being given the opportunities that white coaches were being given. They were granted very few interviews. In August 1987, a meeting was held at Caesars Palace in Las Vegas. There, I first heard about all the challenges black coaches faced. That was a huge reality check for me.

Out of all the members in attendance, I was not only the youngest member but also a kid who had just won the National Championship four years prior. I think the world is great and genuinely believe everyone loves each other. In my mind, I'm thinking, *"What the heck is everyone talking about black coaches not being given the opportunity to coach."* Everything was fine, and everyone was treated fairly. Honestly, I was blind to it all. I was very naive about the world. Again, remember, college is a very sheltered place. It's just not the real world. You don't read the paper or watch the news to keep up with what's happening. You're just a kid in your 20s having fun. Then, I went to Europe to play and became an assistant coach. So, when I joined the Black Coaches Association, I had no idea about anything in college basketball that was racially related. Who knows, always being one of my team's star players kept me from dealing with those situations.

When I first heard Harry Edwards talk about all the racism that was going on and that we all may be losing our jobs, I was very confused. I had been an assistant coach for two years and honestly didn't think we had a problem. It was there when all those conversations I had with Coach Valvano in his office back when I was a player began to make a lot more sense to me. As I was sitting there at the meeting, I began looking around the room, and I noticed that many were fighting for an opportunity to coach. I even wondered how any of what was brought up during the meeting would affect me moving forward. I was happy that I had decided to join the Black Coaches Association because it made me more aware of situations I did not know were taking place. One of the lessons I learned from the meeting was that if there was one thing people need to understand about racism is the fact that if *they* don't have to deal with it, it isn't their issue. It was a critical time for me, and I am proud to say that I was among the first to join an organization that helped black coaches get more job opportunities.

Chapter 17

Valvano's Demise

After coaching at Long Beach State for one season, I received a call from Coach Valvano letting me know he had an assistant coaching position available, which I thought was a great opportunity for me at my alma mater. I accepted the position and now I was back coaching in the ACC. Coach Valvano had been given a lifetime contract in 1986 to be the head coach and athletic director at NC State which was unheard of then. But no matter his success, there were still so many other coaches who really didn't like him. But judging it from the outside, his becoming head coach and athletic director was like a sign of power. If they hated him as just being a coach, imagine how they all must have felt once he had both positions. Not to mention, Coach Valvano had signed a lifetime contract with the university. Now, how many coaches have you ever heard of doing that? Before coming to NC State, he had also been the athletic director and head coach at Iona College; *remember the college he owned?* So, he felt he could do it again. He had put himself in a great position, but it was also tricky.

From the first meeting he and I had, he explained that being a coach was a business and was very different from being a player. He wanted me to understand that although he and I had a great personal relationship that we had to understand, we had to learn to separate the two when it came to working side by side, which I had no problem understanding. I understood I was no longer one of his players, so it was a different light. Playing for him was unique because I had always admired him. But as I began to spend more time with him, I got to know more about him. I got to know more about his family, his work ethic, and his philosophies. I thought he was more extraordinary working for him as a coach than I thought of him when I was a player. It was just two entirely different views of him as a person. Coach Valvano and I had always had a great connection, and we just gravitated to each other because we shared love and respect. I knew it would be an incredible experience. I was just excited to be back at NC State.

Coach Valvano's personality was magnetic! He could always light up any room. I remember going with him to recruit Shaquille O'Neal, and when Ms. O'Neal brought us a Coke, he spilled it all over himself, and we laughed about it. He was just a hilarious person to be around. I remember he was hungry and told me to pull into a Chinese food place in one of the roughest neighborhoods in the DC area. I told him, *"I don't want to pull up in there."* He looks at me and says, "Man' don't worry about anything, *and let's go up in there."* Coach Valvano was the same person everywhere he went. He just lived his life and moved around as if nothing in this world could ever be a distraction to his happiness. That's the kind of guy he was all the time. Remember his speech? That wasn't a speech; that was really him. *"Laugh every day, spend some time in thought, and have your emotions move you to tears."*

Coach Valvano was an English major and was a pretty good basketball player at Rutgers University. He was very smart. He wasn't a conventional coach. He loved to do coaching, but he could talk to you about many things. He loved people, could be funny, and was extraordinarily talented. He was one of the greatest speakers you have ever heard. Let me tell you this: I have been around actors like Denzel Washington, famous athletes, television celebrities, and professional speakers. I have never met another person with more of a magnetic personality than Coach Valvano. His personality could outweigh anyone. If I had put Coach Valvano in a room full of stars, he would have taken over and dominated the room. I have witnessed it for myself many times. They may have stature, but Coach Valvano had personality and charisma. He just knew how to make people feel good. It's very hard to describe in words how he was in person. He was just off the charts. He was just different from anyone I have ever known.

In our first year of coaching side by side, everything seemed to be going very well. We had a pretty good team, and we had accomplished so many great things. On the team, we had Chris Corchiani, now the all-time leader in assists, and Rodney Monroe, the all-time leading scorer in NC State history. I will never forget coaching those guys. After a terrific season, we lost to Georgetown in the 1988-89 NCAA Tournament Regional Semifinal. It was a historical game because we played against the legendary Coach John Thompson and future NBA Hall of Famers Alonzo Mourning and Dikembe Mutombo.

Everything seemed to have been running smoothly for us out on the court during the 88-89 season until I began to hear whispers of a scandalous book that was being written about all the inner workings of the NC State basketball program. From my understanding, this book focused more on the 86-87 season; I was not there when the accusations of corruption were suggested. However, some believed that Coach Valvano had heard about it before I returned to become his assistant coach. Some felt Valvano brought me back because he trusted me, and it was a good look for him to bring me back to coach at NC State.

At first, many publishers didn't want to touch the book because there were so many inconsistencies, innuendos, and accusations that were not true. During halftime of a nationally televised game between North Carolina and NC State, it had been made public that the book entailed information such as players being offered cars, cash, and an apartment by Valvano while still at NC State. The book even went as far as to say that positive drug tests were being covered up so that players wouldn't have to face consequences. I was coaching at George Mason and Long Beach State when all the information was being gathered for the book. I will say this, though. I do know that during the time I had been coaching at Long Beach State, Coach Valvano had gone out to UCLA to try and get the head coaching job there. I'm unsure if he was trying to separate himself from the rumors circulating about his basketball program at the time or if it was because he really wanted to move on from NC State.

The accusations went on for a year and a half. It all started in the middle of the 1988-89 season and carried all the way into the next season. It was also national news the entire time. Before I go any further, remember the timing of all of this. Coach Valvano had won both the ACC and National Championship in 1983 and the ACC Championship in 1987, took the team to the Elite 8 in 1988 and was named ACC Coach of the Year in 1989. Coach Valvano was really doing well. So, there were many people out there who were very jealous of him and all the things he had been accomplishing. After winning the National Championship in 1983, Coach Valvano became a celebrity. There was a high demand for him. He was out doing speeches, on national television every other day, and just out there having fun. The only issue was losing focus as a coach and what's happening around you when you get to that point. And when you're on top, people start gunning for you. Suddenly, you have all this negative news coming out.

Coach Valvano's part of the story has never been told publicly. And although I was there to see him go through the things he did, I'd much rather see the people who accused him of so much wrongdoing and came up with almost nothing to suffer in their own guilt. Because, in the end, what they did to him was wrong. I'm the only one alive who can tell that story on his behalf. I can tell you that those two years were the toughest years of our lives. I remember how the mood changed when the book came out. We all knew that once the book was released, the media would gravitate more towards the negative than they were to the positive. Like some of them do when it comes to accusations, they always multiply on the negative. So now, Coach Valvano was wrongly accused of so many things far from the truth. The majority of what was portrayed in the book were lies and false accusations. But we all knew that most people who read a book would sway more towards believing it because it was all in print. Many people believe it must all be true if it was written in a book. The newspaper never took a day off from printing a negative article about the scandal because it sold papers. It became such a huge scandal that there wasn't a single day that went by when we didn't see it on the news. I could say that we were lucky that it was all happening back then without social media. I can't even imagine what it would have been like had that been going on today.

When the Personal Fouls book was published, the NCAA came in and investigated everything that had to do with NC State basketball. They were investigating summer jobs, what kind of cars the players were driving, and even looking into the game tickets that some of our players had been accused of selling. The book even went as far as to say that there was gambling involved. This was serious stuff. We dealt with this situation daily, and there was nowhere to hide. The book had people thinking all these things were happening behind the scenes. The sad part was that while we dealt with this book situation, many people who had been close to Coach Valvano quickly turned on him. That alone was one of the hardest things he had to deal with. During this time, some NC State players accused of point shaving forced a grand jury investigation in which I had to testify. I was still young and had no idea what it meant to be interrogated by a prosecutor. I remember meeting with Coach Valvano and telling him I had no problem testifying because I had nothing to hide. I told him I would not lie and would tell them nothing but the truth.

Here was a beloved coach who, at one point, had all kinds of people around him. Suddenly, he has all this trouble, and people rush to pass judgment. Where are his supporters? Who's there backing him up? The university is embarrassed that all of this is coming down. The academic department's idea of what Coach Valvano was involved in is now destroying their reputation, and many alums were angry at him. Part of the issue was that people confused his notoriety and star power as his personality, but that was far from the truth. He was really disturbed by everything that was going on. It appears everyone had turned on him. I didn't like how people treated him during this difficult time. By now, Coach Valvano was feeling like he was alone.

The investigation lasted about a year and a half, and we were placed on probation. Once the NCAA got involved, I gathered information about summer jobs and the athletes' cars. They were alleging that Coach Valvano was getting all this money from different summer jobs, paying off the athletes, and paying for their cars. I was responsible for going to every kid with a job and asking them how many hours they worked, how much they were paid, and did you have somebody comparable? I gathered all that information, and, in the end, there was no wrongdoing. I did much of the background work for that information. None of our players had extravagant cars or were being paid extra money on the side for jobs they were working. I knew all the people our players were working for, and I knew all their parents.

Even though all of this was happening, we still managed to stay focused throughout the season and ended up having an incredible year and winning the regular season. It was a trying time for us, especially for Coach Valvano. I could tell it was beginning to destroy him because he knew he wasn't trying to cheat; he wasn't buying any players or giving them any money. It was all just a big lie. But when you're trying to destroy someone's name and reputation, that really hurts. Especially when you know you are completely innocent of everything you are accused of. Being the athletic director, Coach Valvano played it smart and did a very clever thing. As the investigation was taking place, he sanctioned himself before the ruling came out from the NCAA. He took away scholarships, we were not going to go out on the road recruiting and took our team out of the 1989-1990 ACC and NCAA Tournament before they came out with the ruling to try to soften up the blow. He was trying to admit that he could have done something as the athletic director and coach and figured that once the investigation was completed if there were any other punishments, we would accept them as well.

Coach Valvano may have agreed to the athletic director job because it positioned him to decide how he conducted the basketball program. Also, as the athletic director, you are responsible for athletes in 25 other sports programs at the university. Although you have personnel that could handle that, he still had a lot of responsibility. The scandal was only pertaining to the basketball team. No other sports at the university were being accused of any wrongdoing. But had he not been the athletic director then, he would have probably been fired faster.

We constantly reiterated the rules to all the players. The players knew how to conduct themselves. They understood that they represented NC State. We didn't allow the players to run wild. I always go back to the first things I heard Coach Valvano say at the press conference when he first started coaching at NC State. He said, *"I care about you as a person, I care about you as a student, and I care about you as a player."* He truly meant that. He always reminded his players to never bring their personal problems on the court and to never take their problems in the classroom. or their personal lives; they needed to be focused. He constantly reminded the players to make sound decisions.

Ultimately, the NCAA investigated the basketball program, and some players admitted that they had sold their complimentary tickets and some of their equipment gear. Although it was wrong for our players to do so, I bet you could have gone to any college across the country and found players doing the same. Because Coach Valvano was the athletic director and the coach, he was held accountable for his players' actions. According to NCAA Investigator Dave Didion, Coach Valvano was only charged with lack of institutional control.

Coach Valvano came to NC State with a dream and a vision to win a national championship, and he accomplished that. Eventually, he was ousted, but Coach was more disappointed that they had shamed his name. I can tell you personally that I was there next to him every day for those two years; this situation caused a lot of stress in his life. He was constantly worrying about his family, he worried about his team, and everyone else. He was so confident and smart that he thought he could escape anything. But above all, the program now had a black eye on it. It was bad publicity for the university.

Remember that just a couple of years before that book "Personal Fouls" was published, Coach Valvano was the most celebrated coach in the country. Now, he was no longer celebrated. The one thing he told me I will never forget was, *"If there is one thing you never want to happen to you, it is for them to take away your name because your name is all you have."* He said, *"I may have done some things wrong, but I am not responsible for what others do."* It really bothered me to see him that way. And not just him, but his family, too. People forget that part.

While all of this was going on, I saw the writing on the wall and knew that my time at NC State was about to come to an end. Coach Joe Harrington had called me to let me know he was leaving Long Beach State because he had been hired as head coach at Colorado University of Boulder and asked me if I would be his assistant again. Of course, I didn't want to leave Coach Valvano and NC State, but things didn't look good for us there. I knew he would eventually be fired. I went and talked with Coach Valvano and told him I had an opportunity to go to Colorado University of Boulder. He had absolutely no problems with that. In fact, he supported me and encouraged me to go and take the job.

On April 7th, 1990, Coach Valvano was forced to resign as head coach and athletic director at NC State and was replaced by Les Robinson. Many people felt Coach Valvano didn't deserve any of what he had been through. I know he didn't deserve any of it because I was right there with him all along. He was no cheater. He wasn't breaking the rules. He might not have been aware of everything happening, but he was an excellent coach, and no one could take that away. Unfortunately, some of the players failed him. Coach Krzyzewski couldn't have put it any better when he said, *"People fabricated things to bring him down because he not only won, but couldn't stand the way he won, he didn't cheat, and I thought it was unjust that happened to him because it was totally wrong."*

Shortly after his resignation, Dennis Swanson, the President of ABC Sports, called Coach Valvano, and they offered him a job as a commentator. He became a broadcaster for ESPN and ABC Sports, where he would sometimes be paired with Dick Vitale. They worked so well together that they even started calling them the *Killer V's*. It was a great fit for him then, especially because of what he had gone through at NC State. A part of me felt happy to see him commentating on national television even though I felt he should still be at NC State. In a sense, he was like a trendsetter even when he wasn't trying to be one. He transcended many things in terms of what you did outside of coaching. When it came to coaching, it just wasn't the same for him as it was for everyone else. While I was coaching alongside him, I believe he was looking to get into other things besides being a coach. In fact, I truly believe that he wasn't trying to be the head coach at NC State for the next 30 years. After winning the National Championship and becoming the athletic director, he always looked for a new challenge. He was just a different kind of coach, and people were uncomfortable with that. He stood out more than others, and maybe that's what drew so much attention to the point where they were trying to find a way to get rid of him in any way that they could. But the bottom line is Coach Valvano was done dirty. The irony about the entire controversy is that they tried to take Coach Valvano's name away. That is the one thing that he prides himself in the most. And at times, it really felt like the "haters" had succeeded. But in the end, the Valvano name became synonymous with cancer research, a cause that transcended basketball and sports and extended to life itself. Coach won in the end and is smiling down from heaven.

"The one thing I don't like about these accusations and allegations is that they are trying to take my name away from me because if there is one thing you own in this world, it is your name and your word." **Coach Valvano**

Chapter 18

Diagnosed With Cancer

It was now the Summer of 1990, and I was back out west coaching beside Coach Joe Harrington at the University of Colorado. Going to Colorado was a great move and a great experience for me. The fact that Coach Harrington was willing to invite me to coach with him again despite what was occurring with the NCAA investigation into NC State proves that we had a great relationship. Anyone else would have probably tried to keep their distance from anyone near the NC State situation. I loved it in Boulder because it was such a beautiful place to live, and Colorado University was a good school.

Although Coach Harrington and I had a great relationship, the highlight for me during my time in Colorado was meeting and befriending Colorado Football Head Coach Bill McCartney. Bill McCartney was a man grounded in his faith. He was the founder of the Promise Keepers men's ministry, whose mission is mission is to follow Jesus Christ in being a powerful and effective agent of transformation among men in our nation and worldwide. When he was hired as the head coach of the Buffaloes in 1982, the team had a hard time winning games. Coach McCartney had such a unique personality that to turn things around, he hired 4 African American assistant coaches. He was the first head coach to ever do anything like that in that era. To try to build a winning program, Coach McCartney and his assistant coaches came up with the idea to recruit talented players from the inner city who were often overlooked. They went to places like Detroit, Houston, Los Angeles, and Chicago to look for players who could help them become competitors and maybe even win a national championship. Boulder was pretty much an all-white town, so bringing in players from those areas wasn't something that was easily accepted at the time. Jeff Madden, Colorado's strength coach, was instrumental in mentoring the players who had never been in that environment. Before this innovative approach to recruiting players, Colorado had played in four bowl games, losing all four. In 1991, Coach McCartney led Colorado to its first national championship in football by beating Notre Dame in the Orange Bowl.

Winning the national championship was a great accomplishment, but how Coach McCartney and his assistants built the team will forever stay in my memory. Colorado football went from a losing program to becoming the best show in town. Being there for that historic season and meeting great players like Eric Bieniemy and CJ Johnson felt great. Coach McCartney and I built such a great relationship that I did a film on him many years later called The Gospel According to Mac based on what he had accomplished as head football coach of the Colorado Buffaloes in 1991.

Although the basketball team had no championship seasons or made it to the NCAA tournament, working with Coach Harrington at Colorado for three years was a saving grace. The only problem I had with being out west was that I was so far away from my family for extended periods of time. I started flirting with the idea of returning to the East Coast to try and find a head coaching job or even a better assistant opportunity closer to home. While I was in Boulder, I always made sure to stay in contact with Coach Valvano. I would periodically call to check on him. Regardless of what occurred at NC State during the investigation, none changed how I felt about him. I loved and cared about him the same as I always had.

It feels as if it was just yesterday when I heard ESPN commentator Bob Ley break the news that Coach Valvano had been diagnosed with cancer. At the time, I really had no idea what cancer was. The only time I had ever heard anything regarding cancer was during my first season as assistant coach at Colorado. A young man from St. Louis in his early 20s came to work for us as a graduate assistant named Jeff Carlile. He was a great happy-go-lucky kid full of life and everyone liked him. About three to four weeks later, he became very sick. At first, they thought he had the flu. I had gone to his hotel to check on him, but no one knew what was wrong with him. He was eventually diagnosed with cancer. That was my first experience with that terrible disease. Carlile died shortly after being diagnosed. At the time, no one knew what it was or how it came about. I remember asking myself, "What in the world is this cancer thing?"

After hearing the news, I called Coach Valvano to check on him to ensure he was alright. When I talked to him, he was in great spirits like always. You would have thought it wasn't anything serious or that nothing was wrong with him. His attitude and determination were always so tremendous that it left me no doubt that he would be fine. Before hearing the news that Coach Valvano had been diagnosed with cancer, I had been in communication with the late Frank Weedon, who was the Sports Information Director, and with Bobby Purcell, who was the Head of the Wolfpack Club, because I wanted to form a reunion of our 1983 National Championship team.

I will never forget telling Mr. Weedon these two things: for the reunion to happen, Coach Valvano had to be there with us, and we wanted the national championship rings I felt we deserved. We wanted rings like everyone else received when they won because the ones, they had given us looked more like a class ring. Our Athletic Director at that time, Willis Casey, was frugal when spending money. I remember there was a time when Coach Valvano had gone to him to show him nice recruiting brochures that other universities were using. He was trying to persuade Casey to invest in the brochures for the program. Casey looked at Coach Valvano and asked, *"If I get you these brochures, will we win the national championship?"* Coach Valvano looked at him and didn't even say a word. He just collected all the brochures and walked out of his office, but that's how Willis Casey was when it came to spending money. He was a tough athletic director but was also very good at being demanding and competitive. But to Casey's defense, NC State didn't have much money back in those times.

While I was trying to organize the reunion, I told Mr. Weedon and Mr. Purcell that I would not mention anything to the other players until we had agreed on Coach Valvano being present, and we would get our rings. It had been 10 years, and we hadn't seen each other since winning the championship. Not only that, but I also hadn't seen Coach Valvano since I had gone out to Colorado. After finding out that Coach Valvano had been diagnosed with cancer, I really felt we needed to make that reunion happen. In the end, Mr. Weedon and Mr. Purcell agreed to the terms, and we could move forward with our reunion. I did all that behind the scenes for my teammates. We didn't know if the university would allow Coach Valvano to come on campus because they had forced him to resign just 3 years prior. Remember, he went from being a hero one year after winning the national championship to being treated like a villain a few years later. As a player who loved the man, that's hard to take. We know what he went through, but no one ever talks about what his family went through watching him endure those false allegations. Nobody ever talks about that.

The 10-year Reunion was held on February 21, 1993, at Reynolds Coliseum. Until the very last minute, we didn't know if Coach Valvano would attend. As soon as I saw him walking in, I knew he was sick. Even as frail as he was, he still managed to walk onto the court and give a tremendous speech. It was the first time that everyone was able to see first-hand how sick he was. After his speech, he made his way towards the team and greeted each one of us personally. I couldn't believe that when he got to me, he got down and kneeled in front of me. To me, that gesture is the ultimate sign of respect. After winning our games, I planned to hug him the way I always did. But when he kneeled in front of me, I kneeled right back to him to show my respect for this great man, and then I hugged him. Just imagine that for a minute. A coach of that stature kneeling to one of his players. How significant that must have been for the whole world to see. I knew then that I was just as special to him as he was to me.

I truly believe that it all went over everyone's heads. That act of respect and honor between two people was powerful. If you couldn't see how dynamic our relationship was after that, you don't know what a relationship is about. We were paying homage to each other. It wasn't rehearsed. There was a bond between us that I cannot describe.

Coach Valvano

Despite being so sick, Coach Valvano gave a powerful speech at the Reynolds Coliseum that day. He still had such a positive outlook on life and was so confident throughout the entire time he was sick. Honestly, I was surprised when I saw how weak he was. But no matter what, I still thought he would beat it. There was no doubt in my mind that I would see him again. Shortly after our reunion, Coach Valvano was invited to the Espy Awards. Dick Vitale, who had worked with Coach Valvano and had become one of his closest friends, had arranged for him to give a speech during the show. Sometime between our reunion and the timing of the award show, Coach Valvano received the news that he would not live much longer. Because of that, he did not want to attend the show because he had become weaker. When Dick Vitale heard that Coach Valvano was not going to be attending, he called him and told him that he had to do everything in his power to attend. Dick Vitale knew just how important it was for the world to see him on national television. He probably also knew that Coach Valvano wouldn't be alive much longer. Vitale was able to persuade Coach Valvano to attend. It was just a very hard time for all of us.

On March 4th, just 11 days after our reunion, Coach Valvano, aided by Dick Vitale, ascended the stairs at Madison Square Garden and gave one of the most memorable speeches of all time. I watched every second of his speech on television, and all I could do was cry like a baby because I didn't want to believe he was that sick. In fact, he had never told anyone he was as sick as he was. While accepting the Arthur Ashe Courage and Humanitarian Award, he then went on to announce that he was starting up an organization he had named the Jimmy V Foundation for Cancer Research. Shortly after giving his speech at the ESPY Awards, he was hospitalized at Duke University.

Ironically, one of the people who visited him the most was Duke Head Coach Mike Krzyzewski. I say ironically because if you remember when they first began coaching against each other in the ACC, many thought that Coach K really didn't like him. When they were younger, they had played against each other in college. They later coached against each other when Coach Valvano was at Iona, and Coach Krzyzewski was at Army. Coach Valvano was a better player than Coach Krzyzewski and had a winning record against him as a coach at North Carolina State. So, Coach Krzyzewski always wanted to beat Coach Valvano anytime they coached against each other. They were both trying to find their niche while competing against each other in the ACC. Also, the Mike Krzyzewski we know today isn't the same person we knew when he first started coaching in the ACC. He was a very hard-nosed coach who didn't accept nonsense from anybody. However, In the end, the competition created a bond of friendship and respect for one another. They became even closer once it had been announced that Coach Valvano was fighting cancer.

Coach Valvano & Coach Krzyzewski
Photo Credit Ned Hinshaw

In his last days, while in the presence of Coach Krzyzewski, Coach Valvano had begun to write down his ideas for forming the V Foundation. He listed the names of those he wanted to serve as board members. He had appointed me to be one of the members of his newly formed foundation. Coach Valvano never thought he was going to succumb to cancer. He felt he would beat it and that life would go on. He had never portrayed himself as being a guy that had been given a death sentence. He tried doing everything in his power to try and stay alive to the point where he was permitting doctors to try anything they felt would help with his condition. He fought hard until the very end. He never stopped coaching all of us. "Don't give up, don't ever give up" was one of his final instructions to the world. Coach Valvano passed away on April 28th, 1993, at the young age of 47. His funeral was held in Raleigh, North Carolina. I was one of his pallbearers and often visited him at the cemetery.

Coach Valvano not only loved his family, but he also loved people so much that he spent his last days trying to find a way to cure cancer. Although he is gone physically, his spirit still lives on through his foundation. I am happy to say that I am still a part of that. When Coach Valvano started the V Foundation, there was a need for more awareness; there were few fundraisers, and cancer didn't have the attention of enough people. The Jimmy V Foundation took it to a whole different level. Since his passing in 1993, the Jimmy V Foundation has raised over 300 million dollars and awarded over 600 grants nationwide to various researchers and doctors. People are thriving and surviving with cancer due to all the research that has been made possible. This awareness and funding are what Coach Valvano was seeking to do, and I'm honored to be a part of it. Cancer is still the second-leading cause of death. However, in the past 30 years, there have been 3.5 fewer cancer deaths. I believe Coach Valvano would be proud of what the Jimmy V Foundation has done for so many nationwide. I've enjoyed the work of touching so many people because it's such a dreaded disease.

Dick Vitale once said during one of his events that had Coach Valvano never won the national championship, there may not have been a V Foundation. His legacy of fighting against the odds to win a national championship, coupled with his determination to fight and beat cancer, made it possible for his name to bring awareness through the V Foundation. In many ways, it reminded me of the philosophy of using sports to help others, only in this case, it would be to help save lives. In 1995, ESPN developed an annual game called the Jimmy V Classic, where both men's and women's teams play to help raise money and awareness for cancer research. Another great thing that ESPN started was having a Jimmy V Week, which is a way for ESPN to support the V Foundation by raising money and awareness in the fight against cancer. The V Foundation has a 4-star rating as a non-profit organization. Every dollar donated to The V Foundation goes directly to cancer research. The organization's initiative was to raise money and bring awareness to do more research in hopes that one day they find a cure for cancer. Jimmy V week begins on December 1st and ends on December 11th. There isn't another figure in the world who has a whole week dedicated to a cause. The name Jimmy Valvano not only remains intact and survived, but it advanced. Talk about a legacy.

As the story relates, here's what I try to convey to the kids my foundation serves. Think back to the younger me watching Space take a wad of money from underneath his mattress. That seemed impressive at the time. Those types of things can entice a young, impressionable mind. But you never really know what life already has planned for you. It is likely to be much more. I went from a scrappy kid called *"Tweety Bird"* to a National Champion involved in a global research program for cancer research through the V Foundation. That wad of cash under the mattress pales in comparison.

> *"Cancer research may not save my life, but it may save my children's lives. It may save the life of someone you love."*
> **Coach Valvano**

Chapter 19

Back in the ACC

Although I had lost one of my closest friends and mentor, Coach Valvano, I had to head back out to Colorado. Shortly after arriving back in Colorado, my father suddenly became ill. I had already been feeling uncomfortable about being so far away from home. Still, the situation with my father made it more urgent for me to find a coaching job closer to home back on the East Coast so I could be closer to my family. At the time, my parents were still living in Maryland, and when you're so far out west, it takes you almost half a day to get back to the East Coast. Plus, you cannot just decide to drive home at a moment's notice. Traveling that far takes some planning. That's one of the reasons why I so rarely traveled back home to visit.

I explained my situation to Coach Harrington, and he totally understood. My good friend Bill McCartney didn't want me to leave because he felt I had a great chance to become Colorado's next head coach. Although being head coach at Colorado would have been an amazing opportunity, my biggest concern at the time was being closer to my family. I started looking for another job and found a great opportunity as a full-time assistant coach at the University of West Virginia in Morgantown, WV. After the season was over in Colorado, I had a conversation with Gale

Catlett, who was the head coach at West Virginia, about the position. Coach Catlett offered me the position, and I coached at West Virginia for one full season before being hired at Georgia Tech by Coach Bobby Cremins. I did not have anything against West Virginia; I felt coaching there had served its purpose by getting me back on the East Coast, and the opportunity to coach in the ACC at Georgia Tech was too big an opportunity to pass up. Deciding to coach with Coach Cremins was one of the best decisions I had ever made. I learned so much from him as we formed a strong relationship. Coach Cremins had been looking for a good assistant coach after losing Sherman Dillard and felt my experience was a good fit for his program. Still, it helped tremendously that Coach Cremins and Coach Valvano also had a great connection. This connection was such that he felt he knew a lot about me and my work ethic to give me the job. I coached beside Coach Cremins from 1994 until I left early in 1999.

I really loved working for Coach Cremins. He was fair with everyone and had a well-deserved reputation for being a great person to work for. Some head coaches believe you work for them and not with them. Although I worked for Coach Cremins, he made me feel like I was working with him. There was a great deal of respect between us, not only as a coach but as a human being. Other than Coach Valvano, I enjoyed working with Coach Cremins more than anyone else I ever coached with. One of the best things I loved about him was that he always told me how important it was to do my homework and research while I was recruiting. Plus, he always encouraged me to work on my weaknesses because no matter how good we are at something, we always need to work on those things that need improvement in our lives. He was extremely loyal to his people, a trait that has become less common today. Those were just some of the many things I learned while working with him.

Coach Cremins had a reputation for recruiting great guards. While at Georgia Tech, I had the opportunity to recruit and coach one of the best players in the country, Coney Island native Stephon Marbury. In my opinion, he is the greatest high school basketball player I have ever seen. I had never seen a high school basketball player dominate so much as I did during his junior and senior years. He was just phenomenal. He was so good that I knew going in to recruit him that he had his sights set on going straight to the NBA. I thought I needed to recruit two other good guards in case he didn't come to Georgia Tech. If he did not come to Georgia Tech, we would still have another good guard behind him. I will never forget Coach Cremins saying, "No, I don't want you to think about other guards; *just focus on Marbury.*" He didn't want me to focus on anyone except for him. Recruiting Marbury was very special for us at Georgia Tech. I had never seen a kid that was so focused and disciplined. He was the golden child and when our recruitment efforts paid off and he committed to Georgia Tech, I cannot describe our excitement and fulfillment.

Despite having Marbury on our team, our season started off rocky, with a record of 7-7. I remember pulling Marbury off to the side one day and telling him, "You have one foot in the NBA, and you have one foot here at Georgia Tech; the NBA is going to be there for you, but you have to first enjoy this experience, and the most important thing for you to do right now is to play and win with your teammates and listen to the coach." I knew he wasn't fully focused on playing for us. But I also knew he felt he had a point to prove and improve his draft stock. He was ranked the number one high school guard in the country when he came to Georgia Tech. He was one of the greatest high school players in New York City. He was a big deal with a bright future, but I really needed him to focus on the present, and I think he understood that.

When Marbury focused, we started winning, ended up with a 24-12 record, and won the regular season. However, we lost to Wake Forest in the championship game of the ACC Tournament and then to the Cincinnati Bearcats in the Regional Semi-Final game of the NCAA Tournament. We had a hell of a team, but after his first and only year at Georgia Tech, Marbury decided to enter the NBA draft. Marbury was selected 4th by the

Minnesota Timberwolves in 1996. Losing Marbury made it difficult for our team to recover to try and get our program back on track. With Marbury, we had a hell of a team, but losing a player of that caliber was hard to replace. We didn't think he would leave Georgia Tech after playing just one year. This was around when *the one-and-done* or not going to college began to be prevalent. In fact, I remember when I tried to recruit the late Kobe Bryant to come to Georgia Tech and being surprised to hear his father, Jellybean, tell me, "Whitt, I don't think he's going to college," and as it turned out, he was right. Kobe was just that talented. But that period had a heck of a class of kids that made it tough to try and recruit any of them because they were such great players.

I wonder what it would have been like had Marbury stayed with us a few more years. I want to mention that Stephon Marbury was not just a great player, but he came from a phenomenal family. They lived in Coney Island and were such a strong knit family. One of the most powerful things I had ever seen was when Stephon's father, Don, died. He had passed away during a game when Stephon was playing for the New York Knicks. I went to the funeral in Brooklyn, and I had never seen a community as supporting and loving as they were for Stephon and his family. Everyone in the community turned out to pay homage to his father. Stephon's father was a very popular man in the Brooklyn community and was highly respected. He had been very protective of Stephon and had helped make his son's dreams of playing in the NBA come true. I really loved and admired my experience with the Marbury's and their entire family.

It was just an awesome 5 years I spent with Coach Bobby Cremins at Georgia Tech. Aside from my experiences with Stephon Marbury, I also loved working with James Forrest, Drew Barry, Travis Best, and Matt Harpring, who became the school's second-all-time leading scorer. To this day, I still have a great connection with most of the players I coached while I was at Georgia Tech. I really had a lot of fun being an assistant coach at all the universities I had worked for. I learned a lot from all of them and I was able to make a lot of friends who I have remained in contact with to this day. After 5 years at Georgia Tech and 14 years as an assistant coach, I felt it was time to pursue a head coaching position, which had always been my goal.

Chapter 20

Wagner College

In 1999, I saw an opening for a head coach at Wagner College in Staten Island, New York. What attracted me to them was that they had never been to the NCAA Tournament in its hundred-year history. The most notable coach Wagner had was PJ Carlesimo, and the furthest he ever took the team was to the NIT in 1979. So, I viewed it as an opportunity to do something the college had never done before. The funny part about being interviewed at Wagner was that I don't believe President Dr. Norman Smith really knew much about sports. He had no idea of who I was. From my understanding, he saw my resume and asked athletic director Walt Hamline to consider me, and the rest is history.

P.J. Carlesimo with Dereck

I went into the interview very well prepared, and I explained to the committee how I had a 5-year plan and how I was planning to run the program if hired. When I looked around, it seemed they all had this puzzling look, like I was overqualified to coach there. They couldn't believe that I really wanted the head coaching job. I assume they felt that since I had won a National Championship and coached at so many other great schools, I probably could have gone elsewhere and found a better job. I had to explain to them that I wanted the opportunity to coach there because it would be my first head coaching position and that I wanted to be the first coach to take them to their first NCAA Tournament. That interview was very important to me. It was the fairest process I had ever been in. I was hired at Wagner during the summer of 1999. I finally reached my goal of landing my first head coaching position.

To show my recruits how much I truly cared about them, I made sure that I went to their high school graduation. Most coaches weren't doing that. Back then, the purity of the word "student-athlete" was real. As coaches in our organization, we sold education to the students. That was always a priority for me. I also wanted the parents to understand that I would be taking care of their kids to make sure they would become a better person when I sent them back home. That was also very important to me. From day one, I had always guaranteed my players that they would all graduate if they stayed in school. I also constantly reminded them that life wasn't and should never be just about basketball. I wanted my players to always have something to fall back on and not just rely on a dream of making it to the NBA. I wanted to show my kids there was much more to life than being a great athlete. I also wanted to show them that I cared about them. I really wanted them to know that when it comes to life, being a basketball player was just a small part of who they were. I wanted to build young men. The problem with many coaches around the country was that they wanted to circle everything around winning and were probably too afraid to let their kids know that there was a possibility that they weren't going to become professional basketball players. I wanted my kids to live in the moment and enjoy it as much as possible. If they made it to the NBA, great, but in the meantime, I wanted them to focus on the present. I always felt that it's the coach's responsibility to always be realistic with the players, so they don't get too far ahead of themselves thinking about the NBA.

We built the program by recruiting kids from all over the country. I recruited players from North Carolina and DC and kids from all over Long Island, NY. We also recruited Dedrick Dye, who was from Clinton, Tennessee. I recall watching tapes of players I received at Georgia Tech with assistant coach Seldon Jefferson. We came across a tape where Dedrick Dye, who had funny-looking curly hair and was even a valedictorian at his high school, was averaging around 25 points, 5 assists, and 6 steals. After watching the tape, I thought I would bring him on if he could give me at least half of that. My philosophy in building our program was that I wanted to find good students who were disciplined about their schoolwork, had great character, and wanted to win. That was my formula. I didn't care where they came from; that's what I was looking for.

We also had a player named Jermaine Hall from out of Dublin, Georgia, who I had originally planned to recruit at Georgia Tech. I will never forget recruiting him. I received a call from Coach Wallace Prather, an AAU coach in Atlanta, who told me he had a kid for me. So, I flew down and was immediately impressed by Hall. He was a 6'5 power forward, and I knew I had to get him on my team right then. I set up a meeting, then visited his house and discovered that his grandmother was raising him. When I arrived, he had other family members who had heard about me winning the National Championship and wanted to meet me in person. After conversing with them for a few, I remember telling his grandmother, *"I know Jermaine is a really good basketball player and a really good student, but he can't come to New York looking like that."* She looked me dead in my eyes and said, "You know what? I like you, *coach".* And that's how I got Jermaine Hall. Between his grandmother, his AAU coach, and a barber who cleaned him up, we got him to come to Wagner College. Dedrick Dye and Jermaine Hall became our team's two key building blocks.

Then we had Courtney Prichard, who went to South Hampton High School in Long Island. I saw him one day at his school, and he was kicked out of practice. His mother came down and saw me there and said, *"Listen here, coach, you are the right coach for Courtney; I'm sending him to you."* Although he had somewhat of a temper and seemed a little crazy, I wanted to allow him to come and play for us. Fast forward to his junior year, he did well in school and did everything right. But there was this one day when he made me angry. He did something stupid out on the court, but before that, he had been doing things that were building up and making me really upset with him. I went and had a meeting with our assistant coach, and then we called his mother. As soon as we got on the phone, Ms. Prichard said to me, *"Hold up, coach, before you go any further, I know you're probably calling me about Courtney, but I sent him to you, and you can do anything you want with him, but you cannot send him back here, he's all yours."* I had no other choice. He was a little crazy, but in some ways, I liked that. After having a one-on-one with him, he was good. He turned out to be a terrific player. In fact, had he not gotten mad after getting fouled and punching the basket, causing him to break his hand in his junior year, we probably would have won the season that year, too. He ended up missing 5 or 6 games and we ended up falling behind in our record. I wasn't mad about it, though. I was the same way growing up, so I understood his passion.

In our first season, we won 11 games, which wasn't so bad because it was the first year playing together. Midway through my second year of coaching at Wagner, my father passed away on January 11, 2001. Until his passing, I had gone down to visit him during the season which I was grateful for because I had the opportunity to spend some time with him. My father had kidney disease and had been on dialysis for a very long time. The last time I saw my dad was when he was at Prince George's Hospital. He whispered the words "I love you" to me. He had always been such a great father to me. It was a critical time for me because my family was the main reason I returned to the East Coast. During the time I was dealing with my father's passing, I missed one game and then flew back to the university to continue with the season. Of course, I went back to Wagner with a heavy heart and my father in mind, but I know he would have wanted me to continue with my journey of doing what I loved to do, just like the time when he visited me when I was sick before the championship game.

In our second season, we did much better than our first and won 16 games. The third year we won 19 games and made it to the NIT. We just kept improving every year that we played together. In 2003, my fourth season as the head coach, we won 21 games, the regular season, and the conference championship. Jermaine Hall was named Player of the Year in the NEC, and I was named Coach of the Year in our conference. Not to mention that I also managed to bring Wager College to its first-ever NCAA Tournament, which was my goal from the start. We ended up being the 16th seed, and we lost to the University of Pittsburgh, who were ranked number 2 in the country.

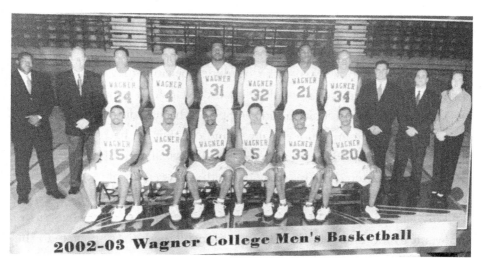

2002-03 Wagner College Men's Basketball

The most significant thing about making it to the tournament was that we played our region in Boston, where we stayed in Cambridge. Making it to the tournament was great, but the highlight was that I took the players on a tour at Harvard. I wanted to take them to one of the world's most prestigious academic institutions and explain why I had wanted to take them there. I always tried to have as many teaching moments with my players as possible. My players had always understood what it was to be a student-athlete. There was never a time when I didn't talk to them about education and how important it was to graduate. Taking them to Harvard was a powerful and significant experience for them. I wanted them to all understand not just the history behind Harvard, but to always remind them that there is always more to life than basketball. I wanted to educate them about as many things as possible. I wanted them to be more than champions in basketball; I wanted them to be champions in life. This, to me, was like the example of Coach John Thompson having the deflated basketball on his desk to remind his players that one day there wouldn't be any air in the ball and sports would eventually be over for them. Coincidentally, Tommy Amaker, one of my best friends, was hired as the head basketball coach at Harvard University in 2007, which I was also very proud of.

At the end of our season, the headlines became that in just 4 years, Wagner College had finally made it to the NCAA Tournament. Wagner President Dr. Norman Smith and Don Spiro, who had donated most of the money to the program, were equally proud of what we had accomplished. But here's what nobody was talking about. It was all about how we ran the program that mattered the most. We kept the players out of trouble all four years. They were all just phenomenal kids. We had an overall average of 3.0 GPA for all four years. I had 6 guys on the Dean's List. But what's most important to me is that I still have a relationship with those players to this day. And all they ever talked about other than winning that year was how they had to dress up in a suit and tie to go to our away games. Many of the other colleges weren't doing that at the time. I got the idea from when I went to DeMatha High School. This was something new to those kids. They hadn't done that before. They never had a coach who made them dress up for their away games. There were also times when I had members of our community come to our games, members from the church come to our games, and members from the YMCA come down to our games. We wanted to embrace the Staten Island community, and we wanted them to embrace our team. Winning was important for us, and we had the ultimate support, but we also wanted them to be proud of the Wagner College program.

My experience at Wagner College was beyond more than just basketball. I wanted to send kids back home with degrees. I wanted to send them back home as better people. I had won all my life. But winning wasn't the thing I was concerned about. It never crossed my mind that we weren't going to win. But I was most concerned about getting my players to do well in school, treat people right, and give me maximum effort when it came to playing basketball. I was always honest with them and reminded them that we weren't talented enough to think we would beat everybody. My philosophy has always been that you must be hungry every game and every practice, outwork everybody and be in better shape, and then apply those principles to everyday life. Many didn't fully understand that then, and I didn't expect them to because they were young. I know they probably thought I was crazy because I was constantly on their ass and pushing them to do better.

Most of those kids knew about my past as a basketball player. Most importantly, their parents knew. But I never needed to throw any of my accomplishments in their faces. To me, it was all about our journey. I always reminded the parents that if they gave me the responsibility of caring for their kids for four years, I would do it right for them. And the icing on the cake was that I would bring them as the first team in school history to the national tournament, which we eventually did. Not only did I take them to the NCAA Tournament, but every player who stayed with me for four years graduated. I had always told my players that a vision is a dream with a plan and that all things are possible, and they all bought in. If you talk to some players today, they will tell you I was tough on them. They might tell you that I was a little crazy, too. I was like that because I understood the challenges they could face throughout their lives. We had a 20-year reunion of our 2003 championship, and they were going around telling crazy stories about me. But, to this day, we still have that special bond. I knew after seeing my former players that my philosophy worked. Today, they are all doing well, and now that they are all adults, they understand what I was trying to teach them while we were together at Wagner College. My four years there was just an unbelievable experience. Aside from the players, I still have a great relationship with Athletic Director Walt Hameline and former Presidents Norman Smith and Richard Guarasci.

When you do something significant at a Division 1 school, you ask yourself, "*What else could I do there?* As was the case for me at Wagner. We had been to the NIT in our third year and then made it to the NCAA tournament in my fourth year. So, in 4 years, we went to two post-season tournaments, which was pretty much unheard of at schools like Wagner. So, I felt like I needed a new challenge. In 2003, I had been trying to renegotiate my contract to stay at Wagner. Still, I saw an opportunity to go after the Fordham University head coach position in the Atlantic 10. What really attracted me to the university was that it was known for its academics. Their basketball program hadn't had much success, but I liked the challenge. I left Wagner and moved on to become the head coach at Fordham University in the Bronx.

Chapter 21

Fordham University

There are times when you get into a situation without knowing how bad it is until you get there. As was the case for me at Fordham University. Their basketball program had been in bad shape for many years. Fordham had only been to the tournament 4 times in their hundred-plus-year history. They went twice in the 50's, once in the 70's when Head Coach Digger Phelps took them to the Sweet 16 and then again in 1992. Back then, Fordham was in the Patriot League. But since then, they hadn't really done anything spectacular after joining the MAAC and Atlantic 10. Aside from that, they had some football history because it's where the great Vince Lombardi played. I understood that and accepted the challenge. I became the head coach at Fordham University in 2003 and was there until 2009.

Fordham, to me, was a step above Wagner College. I accepted the Fordham head coaching position with the same intentions I had for Wagner. I wanted to take them where they hadn't been. When I looked at our team, I didn't think we would win a single game. I only had 5 or 6 scholarship players and 4 or 5 walk-ons. I knew I needed to rebuild the program, so I had to find better players. In our first year, we ended up with a 6-22 record, winning just three games in the conference. Although we didn't win many games, we did show a few signs of improvement. I had a good recruiting class for our second season, and we won double figures. We showed a lot of progress from the year before. We ended the season with a 13-16 record, winning 8 games in our conference, which was a huge jump forward.

The conference was a hotbed of coaches. In our conference, we had the late Coach John Cheney, the head coach at Temple, Coach Phil Martelli at St Joseph's, Coach Karl Hobbs at George Washington, and Coach Sean Miller at Xavier. Our league had many great coaches, so I always knew winning would be a challenge. Not to mention that all those teams were in the top 25 in the country at the time. I got a contract extension during my second season as we headed into my third season. I had recruited a really good player named Bryant Dunston, who was from New York. No one really knew who he was at the time. He was unsung and had great potential as a player. Above all, he was just such a great kid. I truly believe that if I had him today, he wouldn't have gone to Fordham. He would have probably ended up at St John's or another major east coast school known for basketball. He was just that good. We played well that year and won half our games by ending the season with 16-16 and 9-7 in our league, tied for 5th place. Like we had done at Wagner, we just kept improving each year.

In my fourth year, we ended the season with an 18-12 record and tied for 4th in our conference. It was Fordham's best basketball since joining the Atlantic 10. We basically had 3 consecutive winning seasons, which was unheard of at the time for Fordham. Unfortunately, the following two seasons didn't turn out well for me at Fordham. I coached at Fordham for a total of 7 years before being fired. My firing was just two seasons removed from giving Fordham their best two seasons in 25 years, so I thought it was unusual for them to fire me at that time. Coaching is a tough profession. It is a *"what have you done for me lately"* business. One of my proudest moments as the head coach at Fordham was when all my players graduated, just as my players did at Wagner College. We ran a clean program. Many people take that for granted. They only seem to measure things by winning. It's usually never about the player's academic success. To me, that's what college should be about.

When you get fired as a coach you feel humiliated by it. At the time, it felt like the worst thing in the world. Sometimes you can take being fired so personally to the point where you want nothing to do with school. But that's not who I was or wanted to be. Regardless of what had occurred, I still felt great about my experience and appreciated being given the opportunity to coach at Fordham University because we were able to accomplish many great things there. Things didn't work out; how they handled it was just part of the business. I looked at things from a different perspective. Like, what could I have done differently? What better choices and decisions could I have made for a different outcome? But I reached the point where I was past the situation and respected whatever happened. Years later, Fordham had three players, *Juan Gaston, Marcus Stout, and Bryant Dunston,* who had been inducted into the Fordham Basketball Hall of Fame, and I went back there to show my support. That situation was like what Coach Valvano had done for us when he returned to NC State for our reunion. Valvano was a coach who had done well; some things happened, and he was let go. But in the end, he showed he was the bigger person by coming to our ten-year reunion in his last days alive. He didn't show any ill will towards the university. In fact, his showing up proved just how much he loved them and all the fans. I learned a great lesson from watching him set aside all that had occurred and still be man enough to come to our reunion even when he barely had the strength to do so. When it came to my situation, I just found a way to move on from it. I never made one comment in the New York media, where I'm well-liked. I never felt the need to explain to anyone why I had been fired. I ended up leaving Fordham after the 2009 season and taking a year off to try and regroup.

When I was an assistant coach at NC State, Coach Valvano always teased me in his office by saying, "*You want this red chair, you want to be the coach at State?*" meaning become the head coach at NC State. I always responded, "Absolutely, I want to become the head coach at NC State one day; *I would love to have the red chair.*" Around the time I had started to have my issues at Fordham, there had been an opening for the head coaching position at NC State. Everyone around me always told me that after 26 years of doing such a great job with recruiting, having been part of the National Championship at NC State, and having all the credentials I had was enough to become the head coach at NC State, but it never happened. I was truly happy when my long-time friend and teammate Sydney Lowe was hired as the head coach. I hoped to see NC State cutting down the nets again soon.

Chapter 22

The Making of Survive
And Advance

After taking a year off, I was hired to work in the studio and become a color commentator for basketball games on ESPN. I worked there for 3 years until 2013. The strange coincidence of being hired at ESPN was that it was very similar to what Coach Valvano had done once he was no longer the coach at NC State. The only difference was that he had resigned, and I had been fired. During my time at ESPN, Walt Perrin, VP of player personnel for the Utah Jazz, asked me to be on their staff for one year. So, I was basically scouting and commentating games at the same time. I moved to White Plains, NY, because it was much closer to Bristol, Connecticut, where the ESPN corporate office and studios are located. It was an easy transition because I was doing games for the ACC, Big East, and MAAC games on the East Coast. I had a lot of contacts at these schools, and I knew many of the coaches, so the fit was perfect for me. One of the great things about having those two jobs was that I could enter any arena with my ESPN pass. It was cool doing both jobs at the same time. The weird thing about being a commentator at ESPN was that they really don't train you. I did one mock interview with a play-by-play guy, and that was it. They handed me a schedule, and I was alone after that.

Remember, most producers had never played or coached basketball, but their strength is in the production and content of the game. Our job was to provide an accurate analysis of the game in a way that viewers could understand. There were times when I felt like I was a co-producer and a commentator at the same time. Working at ESPN was a great experience because I learned a lot about the production side of television. When I commented, I always wanted to make sure I talked about my experiences as a player and as a coach. What I often provided to the listeners weren't just my opinions; they were facts. Opinions might be great, but most people get into it because of how they feel. It's not about how you think; it's about the truth. Once you state the facts, you can go into how you feel about them. If there is one thing we don't deal with enough in this world, it is the truth. I enjoyed being an analyst because I could give the background on what was happening in the game and explain to the fans why it was happening. I was the funny color guy who shared stories while analyzing the game. I was very comfortable because being a commentator didn't come with as much pressure as being a coach trying to win games. The first game I commentated on was a Wake Forest game. My godson, Travis McKie, was playing for them at the time. I thought it was cool because not only was he my godson, but it was also an ACC game. My second game was at Niagara University, which was also memorable because I came across former Niagara great and all-time leading scorer and Houston Rockets Superstar Calvin Murphy, who was in the stands. I had always admired Murphy because he was such a great basketball player, so I called him for a quick interview about his career. I was very excited to talk to him. I remember doing a skit where I asked Murphy, *"If I'm over in the corner and you have the ball, would you pass it to me?"* He said, *"I don't know,"* and we laughed. Moments like that made being at the games and seeing people like Murphy a lot of fun.

Another great memory from my time at ESPN was working alongside the late John Saunders. He was such a superstar at ESPN. He was from Canada, and many people do not know that he used to be a hockey player growing up. He had been a news director and sports anchor in Ontario before relocating to Baltimore, Maryland, where he started working as a sports anchor in 1982. Eventually, he became the second African American commentator in ESPN history (Greg Gumbel being the first), and he also worked alongside and became good friends with Coach Valvano. Saunders and I developed such a great bond and relationship that I believe was fueled by our great admiration and bond with Coach Valvano. Before I worked at ESPN, he would always come to my Fordham games anytime we played in the New York area. Saunders was somewhat of a pioneer. Everyone looked up to him. Before Stuart Scott and Stephen A. Smith, John Saunders was the face of ESPN. I'm not saying that no one acknowledges him and how great he was as a broadcaster and person, but many people forget what a superstar he was then. Not only was he a huge pioneering star, but while he was there, he helped everybody, including me. We spent time together, and he gave me great advice. He was just such an incredible journalist and had an impeccable memory. He could do the play-by-play on the set and come up with things without hesitation at the drop of a hat. He was extremely brilliant and just so gifted in so many ways.

John Saunders used to be a hockey defenseman in the Montreal Junior Leagues and had also received a scholarship to play at Western Michigan University. His brother, Bernie Saunders, whom I had also befriended, was only the fifth Black player ever to play in the NHL. Through broadcasting, John became very close to Coach Valvano. John and I were a part of the original board members of the Jimmy V Foundation when ESPN and Coach Valvano first put it together after his ESPY Speech. One of my best memories was when they teamed me up with John Saunders to commentate the Rutgers versus Seton Hall game. It was very significant to me because Saunders was a great friend of Coach Valvano, who had played at Rutgers. It was such a great experience and an important moment for me. While I was doing that game, I remember looking up and noticing a banner of Bob Lloyd. Lloyd was Coach Valvano's roommate when they were in college together. He was a great player and finished his career as the second-all-time leading scorer at Rutgers. We also have a great relationship at the V Foundation, so to be able to reference him while calling a game with John Saunders, all of us having such a close relationship with Coach Valvano, made that game very special.

Me with Bernie and John Saunders

The most significant thing for me while working with Saunders was when we were watching the 30 for 30 films on Michigan's Fab 5. At the time, I had a friend, Alex Evan, who worked for *Hock Films* as a producer that I had hired to help me build the first ever website for the athletic department at Fordham University. Building that website costs $50,000 out of our basketball budget. I had done all the content for it and managed it, which was cool and creative at the time. After watching the Fab 5 documentary, I remember telling myself I would call Alex so he could connect me to Johnathan Hock, the director and producer of the documentary on Marcus Dupree, 30 for 30, *The Best That Never Was*. I wanted to connect with Hock because I had a great story about our 1983 NC State team and Coach Jimmy Valvano.

Hock had a great relationship with ESPN due to the 30 for 30 films he had done, and I felt we could make it happen. Once I met with him to go over my idea, he agreed the documentary I had in mind was great. That was my first time getting involved in making a film and going through the process of putting a documentary together. They gave us a budget for the film, but we wouldn't be paying any of the guys who would be in it. We just hoped that everyone would agree to participate. I planned to call all my former coaches and teammates to meet and begin filming. Former assistant coach Ed McLean at NC State passed away during that planning time. After his funeral, I remember telling all my former teammates from our 1983 team who were in attendance that if we didn't get together more often, we would only be getting together at each other's funerals. Just two weeks later, on June 27th, 2011, Lorenzo Charles died in a bus accident. The timing of his death was just horrible because I was maybe about a week away from calling him to let him know about the documentary and how he was going to play a big part in it. Having been connected to Charles for the past thirty years, I now found myself speaking at his funeral. Now, here's an eerie thing about Coach Valvano and Lorenzo Charles. Not only were they buried about ten feet away from each other at Oakwood Cemetery in Raleigh, NC, but they both passed away at the age of 47.

Although we were now missing a major part of our 1983 Championship team with Lorenzo Charles's passing, most players came together, and we began filming the documentary. The great thing was they were all excited about doing it. We interviewed sports writers, some of my former teammates, and many opposing coaches I've had a great relationship with. The 2012 Final Four was coming up in New Orleans. I told John Hock that the only way we would get all the coaches we needed to be in the film was to meet them all there where I could run them up to our room one by one and interview them. That was how we got Basketball Icon Sonny Vaccaro, Head of Adidas Basketball and a longtime close friend of Coach Valvano, on the documentary. Vaccaro is also well known for discovering star players like Kobe Bryant and Lebron James. We were also able to get Lefty Driesell, who was the first coach to win more than 100 games at 4 different Division

1 schools, Roy Williams, who won 3 National Championships at North Carolina, and Jimmy Harrick, who the 1995 National Championship at UCLA, as well as many others who were excited about the film. They were all fantastic and played a major role in the documentary.

In making the documentary, I thought I knew everything there was to know about the story. Still, the big surprise was the relationship that Coach Valvano and Coach Krzyzewski had developed before his passing. It shocked me because they had competed against each other so intensely throughout their careers. They were competitive as coaches but also competed against each other as players during their college years. Learning how they became close while Coach Valvano battled cancer at Duke University Hospital was very special to me. In fact, no one really knows that Coach Krzyzewski was with Coach Valvano when he took his last breath. That really humanized Coach K because it allowed me to see him as a great coach and an all-around great human being. Everything that he said during the interview was authentic. We didn't hand him any questions for him to rehearse, and we didn't tell him what to say. The camera rolled, and he answered the questions. I thought his interview was the most crucial scene of our documentary, and I am very grateful to Coach Krzyzewski for allowing us to tell the story of his relationship with Coach Valvano.

We did the entire Survive and Advance documentary in one take. I knew Jonathan Hock was good, but I discovered how good he was by watching him produce the documentary. We never really knew where the story and interviews would take us. As a matter of fact, I talked to the editor, who was one of the first people to interview me in the documentary. I had never met him before that. During the interview, he asked me questions that seemed as if he was trying to lead me to say certain things that seemed scripted, but that was not what I wanted. I wanted everything to be natural and speak what was in my heart and mind. I just knew what I wanted to do and say for the documentary. In a good way, I just said to him, "Hey man, don't worry about that. I got this, and we all laughed about it. That was just the way I approached many things in my life. We set up the lights, stood before the cameras, and went for it. No one told us what to say or do, and we just rolled. Not a single scene in our documentary was scripted.

The thing about the documentary is that three of our players weren't present at the round table. Alvin Battle, Dinky Proctor, and Sidney Lowe were missing from the round table. Of course, Coach Valvano, Quinton Leonard, and Lorenzo Charles had passed away; I never did ask Sidney nor Battle why they weren't there and didn't participate. When it came to Dinky Proctor, I understood his situation. Dinky, who was part of our 1983 team, had hurt his knee earlier that season to the point where he could not travel with us, which was very traumatic. One thing I can say about him is that he was full of life and was a great teammate. He was just such a great guy to be around. Unfortunately, his basketball career was derailed due to his injuries. Regardless of him not being on the documentary, I will always consider him a great friend and teammate. Regarding Lowe and Battle not showing up, I told myself that the show must go on and that we would roll with what we had, and we did. Let me say this, though: had Coach Valvano been alive today, he would have probably dominated the entire roundtable. In every scene, while at the roundtable, not everyone talked; only the veteran players did. That was the respect that we all had for each other. We didn't tell each other to tell a story. We all just spoke naturally. We did hundreds of interviews and scenes that never made it to the documentary. We had even spent an entire day and a half with Lorenzo Charles' son. The only issue was that there was no place that we could fit that scene in. There was one scene where we reenacted the final play of the championship game where I threw the ball up and his son dunked it, but we couldn't find a place to put it. Although it wasn't added to the film, I still thought it was genius.

After completing the documentary, we tried pitching it to ESPN. The first time we took it to them, they told us they were thinking about it, but there were no takers. We waited for a couple of months, but still no takers. We even tried presenting it to TNT Sports and CBS, but still, no takers.

This back and forth went on for about a year and a half. I decided to talk to a friend, Mike McDonald, who was also a member of the V Foundation and used to play and coach with Coach Valvano back at Rutgers. I explained that I was having difficulty pitching the documentary and he said, *"Why don't you go and talk to George Bodenheimer about it."* Mr. Bodenheimer, who had been working in the mailroom at ESPN when Coach Valvano was hired to work there and was the driver who had gone to pick Coach Valvano up at the airport, was now the president and CEO of ESPN and Disney and was also on the V Foundation Board. So, I met with Mr. Bodenheimer and explained that I had been trying to pitch my film and was having difficulty getting networks to agree to air it. He had no idea what film I was even talking about. No one had even brought it to his attention. He asked me, *"What film?"* I explained that we were trying to do a film about the 30-year reunion of our 1983 National Championship team, and he asked, *"Well, why are we not doing it?"* Miraculously, we got the green light the next week, and that's how Survive and Advance was born.

With Harry Rhoads, My Wife Jaqueline, and George Bodenheimer

I learned a very valuable lesson from that interaction with Mr. Bodenheimer. I learned that I would go straight to the man in charge if I ever needed something to get done. Today, we have more access to the CEO and Presidents than ever imagined. Sometimes, you reach out to certain people that may be on the team, but the messages may never go much further. It took us about a year and a half to complete the documentary and another year to get it on the air. The difference between our documentary and the other 30 for 30 films was that ours was a two-hour film. It was the first two-hour documentary of that series. Although they had already reached the 30 films related to the 30 documentaries, which was the original intent and inspiration for the 30 for 30, they decided to keep the theme and continued producing films. It was an incredible journey going through the process of finally getting our story to air. Survive and Advance finally aired in March of 2013, coinciding with the 30th anniversary of our championship run, revitalizing the moment all over again.

Before launching the film to the public, we did two premiers. One at Reynolds Coliseum at NC State and the other at the Umstead Hotel in Cary, a private show for NC State donors. After seeing everyone's reaction, that's when I knew the impact of the film. At the Umstead hotel, we had about 200 of our top donors who were friends of Coach Valvano and the Valvano Family there watching it. The emotion in that building was like nothing you had ever seen before. It just touched them and reduced many of them to tears. I had never seen that kind of emotion from an audience before. Everyone there was crying. The Valvano Family, who were also in attendance, appreciated the film; that meant the world to me knowing they had approved it. Truthfully, I believe that changed peoples' perception of Coach Valvano and made them appreciate his accomplishment of creating the Jimmy V Foundation. You must remember that Coach Valvano had been wronged for so long and now this film brought all the goodwill back. Never in my life would I have imagined that the documentary would have turned out as great as it did. I had no idea what it was going to do or where it was going to go. It's just like this book. I just wanted to share my story. I wanted to share our story and tell the story of everyone involved. John Hock did such a masterful job on the documentary. Survive and Advance became the most-watched sports documentary in the world and the first to ever receive an Emmy Award.

Me with John Dahl and Jonathan Hock

After the Survive and Advance film, we filmed *The Gospel According to Mack,* a two-hour documentary on Colorado Head Football Coach Bill McCartney, whom I had mentioned earlier in this book. That, too, became one of the best and most powerful films in the 30 for 30 series but was not nearly as successful as Survive and Advance. I believe that America wasn't ready to deal with the message the film was attempting to deliver. One of the things I loved about Coach McCartney was that he didn't shy away from controversy and had no problem exposing how the Black athlete was being treated and that he, as a coach, would be nothing without The Great Black Athlete. He caught a lot of heat for that. His delivery may have been lacking, but I know what he meant. What he was saying was very true. Would I have said it that way? Probably not. But I understood him, and all his players loved him. Here was a coach who was a pretty religious guy; his daughter was having a relationship with his quarterback, and he was being persecuted and being called a hypocrite. Still, none of those things ever stopped him from getting his point across.

After John Saunders had seen that Survive and Advance and The Gospel According to Mack had become so popular, he and I came up with the idea of doing a documentary on Willie O'Ree, the first Black hockey player in the NHL. The film was going to expose the history of racism against Black players in hockey, dating all the way back to the 1800s. Unfortunately, Saunders passed away unexpectedly on August 10, 2016, and without his leadership, the film never came to fruition. John Saunders is someone who I think about all the time. He was very special to me, and I miss him dearly.

At the end of the Survive and Advance documentary is a picture of me resting my head on my mom's shoulder. She passed away on February 5, 2013, while filming the documentary. Since 2011 she had been living near me in the White Plains area after my father had passed away. I purposely had her funeral on February 15th because my father's birthday was the day before on February 14th. I wanted to celebrate his birthday and her celebration of life service around the same time.

My Parents ❤

I thought it was great for her to have lived close by because it gave me the opportunity to spend a lot of quality time with her before she passed away. It was always difficult for me not to be able to see my parents while I was off playing basketball in college in North Carolina and then Europe for a year, and then when I came back, I began my coaching career. My career made finding the time to visit with them very difficult. I could always visit them during the holidays, but I didn't see my family as much as I would have liked. I miss my parents, but they are both happy for all I have accomplished. They were both the greatest parents anyone could have, and I loved having them in my life. They did such a great job as parents. I think about them every day.

Working at ESPN was a year-to-year contract. I had reached the point where I really didn't know if I wanted to continue being a commentator. I really enjoyed the games, but it wasn't as stimulating as I thought it would be. When commenting on the games, you must wait for the play-by-play announcer. You then quickly talk about the game, and it's over a couple of hours later. So, when you have been used to playing and being a coach, you're involved in every play. The story was the game when I went to the arena as a commentator. At the end of the day, all the notes I had taken and all the studying I had been doing leading up to the games were pretty much irrelevant. So, it started to get a little boring and lonely for me. You're away from home for two days just for a two-hour game. Then, after the game, everyone just went home or off to their next job. We didn't hang out with the coaches or players like I did when I was playing or coaching. I can't even sit here and mention many of the people that I worked with because, after the games, we would all go in different directions.

Around this time, I received a phone call from Mark Gottfried, who was now the head coach at NC State and had also worked for ESPN. He mentioned that Marc Farmer, the player development coach, had moved on and wanted to know if I could find him one of the former players who might be interested in the position. I had just finished the Survive and Advance documentary, and he asked me, "Would you be interested in the position?" He wasn't interested in anyone else; he wanted me to take the position. After speaking with him, I told him I might be interested, and we hung up. We spoke about it again a couple of days later, and he offered me the position, which I accepted. I left ESPN and was back at NC State in July of 2013. I took over as the player development coach for two years. After notifying the university that I no longer wanted anything to do with coaching, they hired me as the Ambassador Associate AD for Student Affairs and Community Relations. I know that when I was hired, there were probably a few people who felt I was bitter about my teammate Sidney Lowe getting the head coaching position over me or for what the university had done to Coach Valvano. All I can say to those people is to ask yourself this question: if I were bitter, do you really think I would have gone back as the Player Development Coach or as the Ambassador Associate Athletic Director if that was the case? I have and always will love NC State.

Chapter 23

Take Your Shot

Many of us underestimate our support system and what we've learned throughout the years, especially from our parents. The basis of who we are, and the character built along the way comes from them. As I reflect on the beginning of when I was just a young kid trying to figure out what life was about, I have to say that I was very blessed to have two of the most beautiful and influential people one could ever have in my parents. There was never a time when I could say they weren't there for me or lacked in any way as parents. Especially when they made the sacrifice to send me to DeMatha High School. They had made that decision when I didn't fully understand how it might have affected our financial situation at home, but they made it happen. That decision became one of the most important to me because it was the one that helped create the path that led to many other great opportunities along my journey. Although sports became my focus and it sparked such a great interest which I turned to and loved, there were so many other valuable lessons I learned while I was a student there.

I remember when my parents decided to move from DC and how it changed my life. I had no idea about politics or race back then, but my parents weren't running away from those issues. They were looking for better opportunities and a safer environment to raise us. I'm happy that they made that decision rather than trying to teach me how to deal with or defend myself when it came to racism or violence. I thank them because they allowed me to see the world for what it was as I saw it through my own experiences so that I could formulate my own opinions on how to deal with many of the situations I faced. And of course, I didn't know it then, but basketball eventually became my avenue to get me to where I am today. Although I would have loved to make it to the NBA, that wasn't part of God's plans. I took a good situation and turned it into a greater opportunity. I accepted my years as a basketball player for what it was and then learned to use it to help others. That's what it was all about.

Having the opportunity to play for the great Coach Morgan Wootten at one of the top basketball programs in the country meant a lot to me. Coach Wootten was such a wonderful man who taught me many great things outside of what my parents and other relatives taught me. He came into my life when I lacked the discipline I needed to grow as a player and a person. Although winning was important, he taught me to be patient, be a great teammate, and, most importantly, be a leader. His philosophies on playing the game and all the advice he gave me as a coach were valuable lessons that could have also been applied off the court. Playing for Coach Wootten helped me to accomplish my goal of getting a scholarship to North Carolina State University.

Morgan Wootten taught me about leadership and teamwork early in high school. That's when I learned that relationships were very important to have. The journey of our 1983 team taught me about attitude, perseverance, and how to overcome because I went through so many trials and tribulations throughout that year. Many lessons in those moments helped me grow into a man and be who I am today. I never grew up wanting to be like anyone other than Dereck Whittenburg. I wasn't like most kids today who want to be like Lebron James. I might have said I wanted to make it to the NBA, but there was nobody out there that I wanted to portray myself as other than myself. I can't pinpoint or give you the blueprint and tell you how that developed other than becoming comfortable just being myself. I was like that growing up and am still the same way today. It's not just necessarily telling people what's on my mind; I can articulate where I'm going and where I want to be. Anytime you try to be like anyone else, you lose who you are.

Overall, I am blessed to have many great people in my life. That, to me, is what life is about. Between the teachings of my parents, the hard work and dedication from my schoolteachers, and the guidance and advice from all the coaches that I had along my journey, I have to say this: I would not be where I am today had it not been for the love and dedication that they gave me. They all taught me the definition of what love truly means. Because of them, I could follow their path, wanting to help others. Many of us take for granted all the people we meet throughout life. It's not until we become adults that we better understand why they pushed us the way they did. I tell students and athletes all the time that if they are ever blessed to have good people around them to learn to appreciate them because they may see something in you that you aren't able to. Although I knew I was a good athlete growing up, it took for Ms. Osborne to see through her vision the potential that I had. That was a pivotal moment in my life.

Everything I had accomplished before graduating from NC State became chapters in my life. I went to one of the most prestigious high schools in the country and won the championship. I went to a major university and won the national title. Most importantly, I became the first to graduate in the Whittenburg Family, which greatly benefited me. After graduating from NC State and realizing that I would not be playing in the NBA, I never allowed that to deter me from continuing to find the next chapter of my life, which is what I believe we all struggle and strive to find in our lives. I quickly learned that there were more dreams and more things to accomplish outside of wanting to play professional sports. From there, I had to figure out my next chapter and what I wanted to achieve for the rest of my life. In terms of each chapter from high school to college and having the opportunity to play professionally, I had maximized those three things as far as I could, and my next chapter was in coaching.

NC State graduation 1984 Terry Gannon and I

I had the opportunity to coach with and for many great mentors like the late Jimmy Valvano, Bobby Cremins, Joe Harrington, and Gale Catlett, who all gave me the opportunity and made it possible to eventually become a head coach. Without them, I probably would have never gotten that opportunity. When I decided to become a head coach, I wanted to go to a school where I could have an impact. Becoming the head coach at Wagner College and Fordham University became a great opportunity for me to do something those schools had never done before.

I've always looked for truth, transparency, and trust in people because it is within that journey that people will reveal their authentic selves. Although none of us are perfect, we want others to experience us as fair people, someone who loves people and is willing to help others, which is the basis of coaching and leadership.

Life should be about those who have positively impacted your life and positioned you to help others. What I love about my journey is that I've built life-long relationships everywhere I've worked and in the community on boards I've served on. For example, helping raise millions of dollars for the V Foundation for Cancer Research is one of the greatest experiences of my life because the foundation has funded cancer research for talented scientists working diligently to cure cancer. Being part of an organization focused on saving lives is a wonderful feeling.

Everyone talks about relationships, but for them to mean anything, you must feel that connection. For example, Joe Harrington and I are still in communication to this day. I still talk to all the people at ESPN. I am still in contact with most of the players I coached from Colorado. I keep in touch with all my players from Wagner College. I stay in touch with many players from NC State. I have always stayed in contact with my Le Mans France coach, Kenny Grant. I am living proof that no one accomplishes anything alone. So, in every chapter of my life, someone was there to add value.

Building great relationships is important because you can get many things done together. I come from a place where people helped each other. Throughout my journey, I have learned that people today are becoming more independent, which makes it more difficult for them to be successful. It is very difficult to get to that next level without help.

Throughout my journey, I earned my college degree, helped win an NCAA National Championship (teamwork), experienced success as a coach, contributed to an Emmy award-winning film, am a motivational speaker, and am now an author. *I am one of the 99% of people who became successful without being in the entertainment industry or a professional athlete.* That's what I always talk to kids about. They all sit there looking around, saying to themselves, "*Who the heck is Dereck Whittenburg, and why did they bring him in here?*" But if I ask them how many think they will become entertainers or professional athletes, some will raise their hand. I constantly reminded them that 99.5 % shouldn't count on it happening. I wanted them to understand that life doesn't end; they have many more talents other than being an athlete. Is it the only thing you can do? Are you just going to give up there?

I've had many great experiences and have accomplished many great things throughout my life. Because of Coach Valvano and my teammates from the 1983 national championship team, I experienced one of the most significant sports moments in history. I have learned from that that in most cases, you not only have to work together as a team, but you must always be willing to take your shot. I've taken many shots throughout my life. I took my shot with Coach Valvano on helping him find a cure for cancer with the V Foundation, I've taken a shot at building a foundation that allows juniors and seniors to finish college with lower student debt, and I've taken a shot at powerful relationships where we try to help others through their journeys. I will continue to take more shots. Even the shot I took in the 1983 Championship game, which I obviously didn't make, shows you that we all must take our shot. Think about it: where would I be today had I not taken that shot?

I focus on how I can help the 99% of people I encounter. I'm working on my legacy of empowering people. That's what I'm working on. I've done all I could in my personal life to earn a living. However, the principle behind all my achievements is to continue to help as many people as possible along the way. I have explained my views, but what are yours? And not only your opinions of this world, how you started, and where you are today, but what will you do to make it better? It all starts with you. How are you going to be better? How are you going to get out of your comfort zone? How will you take your contact list and have it more diverse? How are you going to help someone else other than yourself? How are you going to impact people with what you want to achieve? What will your legacy be when it's all said and done? There is much more to life than big houses and fancy cars. What else will you do to help somebody before leaving this earth? Those are the questions you should ask yourself. That, to me, is the purpose of this book. I want the 99% to know that "you can do it."

My life came down to that one shot, not just a moment in time, but a split second in sports history. That moment is remembered alongside other great moments in sports history like Tiger Woods making that miraculous chip on the 16th green at Augusta, Michael Jordan's final shot as a Chicago Bull, or even the Miracle on Ice in hockey with Jim Craig draped in the

American flag. When Carly Simon came out with her hit "You're So Vain," she then spent most of her life with people asking her questions about who "that" person was in the song. In the same way, I have spent a lifetime with people asking me about the "shot" or talking about the "shot." So, let's talk about the shot because I think it is an excellent metaphor for life.

First, if you polled the other players on our team, most would either say they wanted the ball to go to me or expected it to go to me. That doesn't happen by accident, and I want to return to this point. But before exploring that idea, let's talk about our great team, an athletic version of an organization. Everybody on our team had an important role, so we succeeded. The final second shot is the glamor part of the story, but the last second shot is not the whole story. I will give you one example of many. Think back to when Terry Gannon stripped the ball away from Sampson. That play was as crucial to our journey as "the shot," but no one speaks about it because it is less glamorous than taking the final shot in a game. But our team consisted of players willing to do unglamorous things to win basketball games. Although I was one of the players that one would expect to take the shot, we had the type of team where any other player would have succeeded in that moment if the ball hadn't come to me. When I think about my foundation, as an example, I am the face of the foundation, but it is the work of so many other people that makes things happen. Our march to the championship comprised great plays and unsung heroes working together. Our team needed to be on that floor to take that shot, and hundreds of unsung plays contributed to our success.

In my case, preparation was essential for that moment. My role was a shooting guard, and I took thousands of shots in formal and informal situations to prepare myself for that moment. In a way, my entire life was preparation for that moment. That is why I am so grateful to all my teachers and mentors. My point is that when that moment came about, I did not hesitate. I prepared for that moment, and more importantly, I wanted it. I expected success when I put that ball up in the air. There was no doubt that I would come through for my teammates.

The most important thing about the shot is that it was a shot. I wanted to be in that moment, and when I put that ball in the air, I had a full expectation that the ball would swish through the same netting that our team would cut down moments later. Once again, I prepared, and the team prepared. But life doesn't work that way. As prepared as I was for that moment and confident in my abilities, life throws us curve balls. Life isn't a linear walk from point A to point B. I have never believed that what happens to you in life is what matters more; how you respond to what happens is what matters most. Everything was working towards the climax as if scripted in a Hollywood movie. Remember, Coach Valvano, let us play rather than adjust to their adjustment. That was brilliant because Coach Valvano always had an answer to the opposing coach's chess move but decided to let us play. So our team played a little street ball, which engaged our basketball instinct, and we nearly lost the ball a couple of times, but the ball eventually came to me for "the shot." And Tweety Bird from DC launched that ball as part of his destiny, and I missed it. I missed the shot. But remember what I said: life is not a through line to success. God had another plan.

In our case, Lorenzo Charles changed the moment by battling beside Hakeem Olajuwon to grab that errant ball and dunk our team to NCAA and sports history. I think of that play in the same way that I think of Coach Valvano's story. It is an unlikely story of an Italian from Queens, NY, winning a National Championship at NC State with a pack of scrappy multiracial kids. But don't you get it? That isn't the story. Coach made a big name, and some people felt he had become too big. So, they tried to take his name away. Coach went from the peak of the mountain to pariah almost overnight. It was like me missing that shot. But here is the beauty in life. The "real" story is "Jimmy Valvano," which has become synonymous with cancer research. That once-tarnished name is now making such a significant impact on cancer. That, my friends, shows how life is not a through line. It is such an important message that I tried to convey to my players and what I try to ingrain in my students from my foundation. Life is that flat basketball like the one in Coach Thompson's office. I tell my kids to put everything that they have into their chosen endeavors but, at the same time, also realize that their success may come from a very different avenue. Think about Barack Obama. I am sure that he had NBA dreams at a certain point in his life, but then he had to "settle" for being America's first black President. That is what I love about that shot! But there is a misconception about the "last shot." People assume that it was my last shot. No, that could never be true for me. As I mentioned, I tried to get into the NBA but that just was not my destiny. At that point in my life, I could have wallowed in self-pity and lived my life in the past centered around our championship at NC State. But that is not in my Whittenberg DNA. I am still shooting, and I am going to keep on shooting. I am involved with one of the world's greatest organizations that is taking shots at eliminating cancer. Through my foundation, I am taking shots to help deserving college students. At the *Dereck Whittenburg Foundation, we are extending hands of financial assistance to deserving college students who* face the hindrance of finance as the barrier to their completion of college degrees. The mantra of The Foundation is "Dream. Believe. Work. Now Finish!" I can't wait to see my students' shots in life. I will continue representing NC State, shining a light on one of the greatest academic institutions in our country. I am going to keep taking shots against racism and social injustice in the world. I will keep producing, writing, and speaking to inspire others.

Dedication

I dedicate this book to the many people who have played a significant role in helping me throughout my journey, especially my great-grandparents, John and Julia Faucett, my paternal grandparents, Don and Solona Whittenburg, my mother's brother, George Hubert and his wife, Mary Hubert. To my parents, Don and Lillian Whittenburg, who laid the foundation, opening doors of opportunity for me to accomplish so many great things. Without them, I would not be the person I am today. There isn't a single thing that I would go back and change in the way they raised me, and I will forever cherish every second they were in my life.

I want to thank my Aunt Ida Bass, Uncle Jay, Aunt Katie, Uncle Dewey and Aunt Mary, Aunt Dollie May, Uncle Adel, Uncle Henry Hubert and his family, my brothers Reginald and Stephen, my sister Wanda, and the rest of the Whittenburg Family. Thank you to Tiffany Johnson, who is like a daughter to me and my godson Travis McKie.

The Family

A very special thank you to my wife, Jacqueline, for all her love and support, which goes unmatched. We have been together since the beginning of my journey at NC State, and we have been together ever since. Behind the scenes, she has been my most vital and valuable relationship. The loyalty, respect, and friendship we've had for the past 44 years is a true sign of our love for each other. I especially thank my late mother-in-law, Annie Mae Williams, and her family for their tremendous support.

With my Wife Jaqueline at the White House

I want to give a special acknowledgment to my neighborhood friends, especially John and Pat Osborne, who were there from the beginning when I played at the Boys and Girls Club. Thank you to Coach Brown, Coach Harry Carter, Coach Herb Gray, Coach Rocky, Coach Cash, and Coach Swindell. Thank you to all the board members at the Boys and Girls Club and all the members of my Boys and Girls Club baseball, basketball, and football teams. To my junior high gym teachers, Mr. Waunslack and Mr. James Tucci.

To my DeMatha High School Coach, the late Morgan Wootten, and his wife, Kathy, thank you for teaching me about life and for teaching me not just the fundamentals of basketball but also how vital life is after basketball.

With Kathy Wootten

Thank you to Principal John Moylan, my science teacher Mr. Conyers, Coach Buck Offutt, Coach Perry Clark, Coach Jack Bruen, James Brown from CBS, classmates Neil Carr and June Wood, Father Damian, Father James, to my longtime special friend and teammate Sidney Lowe, The Adrian Branch Family, Daryl Greene and to all the members of the 1978 DeMatha High School National Championship Team. Thank you to Adrian Dantley for teaching me how to work on my game. Thank you to Senator Tommy Broadwater and Family, Guy Black and Family, Larry Coleman and Family, and Archie Talley and his Family.

To my NC State family, thank you to Coach Norm Sloan. Thank you to Coach Jimmy Valvano for teaching me the importance of a positive attitude and pursuing my dreams. Thank you to Coach Everett Case and his teams. Thank you to my assistant coach, the late Ed McClain. To my cousin David Thompson, thank you for paving the way for me to come to

NC State. Thank you to Al Heartley, the first African American athlete awarded a basketball scholarship at NC State. Thank you to Irwin Holmes, the first African American to graduate at NC State. Thank you to Lou Pucillo, who played under Coach Everett Case. Thank you to Monte Towe, Marty Fletcher, Ray Martin, Beverly Sparks, Francis Combs and Family, Phil Spence, and Family, Pat Koballa and Family, Dr. Wandra Hill and Family, Dr. Clarence Witherspoon and Family, Dr. Clark and Family, Dr. Jack Wilson and Family, Registrar Joanne Byrd, Dr. Joe Hobbs, Dr. Joe Brown, Dr. Thomas Conway, Dr. Don Reibel, Cheryl Boswell, Crockett Long, Anthony Blackman, Benny Moore, Meredith Phillips and Family, Bruce Hatcher, Dr. Beasley, Tom Cabanniss, Jim Rhebok, Strength Coach Wright Wayne, Hawkeye Whitney, Kay Yow and Family, Al Masella, and Family and Kevin Howell. Thank you to my longtime friend, the late Tab Thacker. A special thank you to George and Snooki Hall for giving me my first-ever job and including me as a member of your family. I appreciate everything that you guys ever did for me. A special thank you to all the 1983 National Championship Team members for allowing me to be myself and for the incredible journey for the past 40 years.

Thank you to Coach Joe Harrington, Coach Bobby Cremins, Coach Gale Catlett, Coach John Thompson, Coach John Chaney, Coach Bill McCartney, Coach George Raveling, Coach Tommy Amaker, Coach Seldon Jefferson, Perry Clark, Harry Edwards, Kenny Grant, Walt Hameline, Coach Alex Groothuis and Family, Coach Herman Heard, and Coach Bob Wade. A special thank you to my mentor, father figure in Raleigh, United States Olympic Track and Field Coach, George Williams. A special thank you to Coach Krzyzewski for advising me on how to run a successful college program.

Thank you to all my former players that I coached, starting with Stephon Marbury, Deion Glover, James Forrest, Tom Gugliotta, Nate McMillan, Rodney Monroe, Chris Corchiani, TJ Warren, Trey Jones, Ralston Turner, Cat Barber, Drew Berry, Jermaine Hall, Dedrick Dye, Tyon

Carroll, Marcus Stout, Brian Dunston, Cory McCray, Donnie Boyse, Poncho Hodges, Beejay Anya, Cornell Mann, DeAnthony Langston, Chris Washburn, and Kevin Anderson. Thank you for all the great memories on the court. I wish you and your families many blessings. Thank you to all the parents who allowed me to be a part of their sons' lives as both a coach and a mentor.

To my ESPN Family, I thank my dear friend, the late John Saunders, for mentoring me and helping me in my commentating career. John was more than a dear friend; he was my brother. Thank you to George Bodenheimer for showing me tremendous leadership during my time at ESPN and on the V Foundation Board. Thank you to Dick Vitale for your inspiration and your mentorship and guiding me throughout my commentating basketball career.

Dick Vitale

Thank you to Jonathan Hock and Alex Evans for allowing me to tell the story about our NC State 1983 National Championship Team. You two are truly excellent directors of film. Thank you to Keith Clinkscales and Dan Spears for your years of friendship.

To the Jimmy V Foundation Board Members, Nick Valvano, Harry Rhodes, and Mike MacDonald. Thank you to all the members and volunteers who have been there since it started in 1993. Thank you for allowing me to contribute to an incredible team that has kept Coach Jimmy Valvano's legacy alive. To the Dereck Whittenburg Foundation board members, Leon Cox, Allan From, David McGee, Ron Holanek, Michael Dannar, Guy Black, Brandi Gerew, Jacqueline Whittenburg, and all the DW Foundation Volunteers and participants for making it possible for the DWF to help students attending North Carolina colleges and universities graduate with lower student debt. Thanks to Greg Hatem, Simon Griffiths, Tim Peeler, ESPN, DeMatha High School, George Mason University, and Wagner College for all the great pictures.

To my special friends, Joe Marley and Family, Derick and Sally Close, The Valvano Family, John Nunnally and Family, Greg Hatem and Family, Wendell Murphy and Family, Tom Cabaniss, Larry Woodard, Becky Bumgardner, Michael Finn, Gene Corrigan and Family, Andre Colona, Gus and Doris Gusler, Robert Corprew, and Family, Doug Doggett and Family, Peter Pappas and Family, Mike McDonald, Joe Cantafio, DD Hoggard, Dewayne Washington, Timothy Humphrey, Steve Cronin, Charlie Britt, film producer BK Fulton, Staton McIntyre, Dr. Victor Avis and Family, Guy Epstein, and Family, Former Fordham University Athletic Director Frank Mclaughlin, New York sports writer Al Coqueran, A special thank you to Wagner College President Emeritus Dr. Norman Smith and the late Father Joseph O'Hara, Fordham University, for affording me an opportunity to be a Division 1 head basketball coach. A special thank you to my book team. Thank you to Mr. Kelly Cole, Luis Martinez, John Nunnally, Greg and Missy Alcorn, Bernie Saunders, and Jacqueline Whittenburg.

Notable Accomplishments

I'I'm in the DeMatha Hall of Fame as a team member, the NC State Sports Hall of Fame as a member of the 1983 National Championship Team, and the Washington DC Sports Hall of Fame as an individual. I Won the Baltimore Civic Center Slam Dunk Contest in 1978, MVP of the Western Regional Finals in 1983, MVP of the 1983 Championship Game, and All ACC Performer in 1983. Drafted by the Phoenix Suns in 1983. Emmy Award Winning executive producer of 30 for 30 ESPN documentary "Survive and Advance." 2003 Coach of the Year at Wagner College, 2005 Coach of the Year at Fordham University. I received the John Saunders Courage Award from the V Foundation for Cancer Research, and I was the Commencement Speaker for Computer Science at NC State in 2016.

Rest in Peace to Ms. Pat Osborne, who passed away as I wrote this book. She passed away on October 2, 2023, which also happens to be my birthday. I will never forget the important and pivotal role that she played in my younger years, and I will forever cherish all the memories we shared throughout our friendship.

Made in the USA
Columbia, SC
07 February 2025

53462980R00124